D1264746

JACK-KNIFE COOKERY

E·P·DUTTON & CO. INC.
1852
1952
CELEBRATING 100 YEARS OF PUBLISHING

JACK-KNIFE COOKERY

BY

JAMES AUSTIN WILDER

Profusely Illustrated with Line Drawings by the Author

NEW YORK

E. P. DUTTON & CO., INC.

First Printing . . . May, 1929
Second Printing . . May, 1929
Third Printing . . Sept., 1930
Fourth Printing . . . May, 1937
Fifth Printing . . January, 1946

CONTENTS

JACK-KNIFE COOKERY

CHAPTER I

JACK-KNIFE COOKERY

WHAT can a jack-knife, only a jack-knife, accomplish as a kitchen utensil?

What is Jack-knife Cookery?

This book might have helped Robinson Crusoe some had he not been blessed with a ship-load of tools of all sorts, pots and pans, spade and pick-axe to work with. What if he had just squeaked ashore with only that one valuable implement . . . a jack-knife?

Would he have gone hungry? Not for long, I hope, for he seems to have been quite a "handy man" and would have made his jack-knife do what most American boys, cast away on an island far, far from home, *a desert island,* would try to do as well—with only a sharp and stout knife. Of course lots of good things to cook . . . that is understood.

But we must have a Desert Island. These are always so far away, somehow, that we will be obliged to use a lot of imagination. Any place out of town where there is room to breathe deep The field, the forest, rocky places and the sand.

A Desert Island

Hardest of all to manage . . . mud. Rain, sometimes, sometimes the parched desert with

A Perfect Paradise

only your canteen of water, every drop precious. But often, very often, in our fair land, luckily, a

HELPFUL IN AN EMERGENCY

perfect paradise of a Desert Island with lots of wood, of the right sort, lots of good water, blue sky, green grass, good things to cook and a terrible appetite.

That is the Desert Island we are looking for. Here we can practice the art and science of Jack-knifery against the day when we are really "cast away" a thousand miles from anywhere.

Mostly, however, this shipwreck cooking . . . with camping thrown in to increase the fun, is just for fun. At a picnic. Once in a while Jack-knife, or Desert Island or Robinson Crusoe cooking, which is cooking without a pot or a pan, comes as part and parcel in a PANIC . . . and that's why boys want to learn it . . . to be helpful in an emergency.

My cooking schools in Jack-knifery were scattered and I confess to the following.

1. South Sea Island Cookery: the cuisine of the lovable Kanakas. Hawaii, Samoa, Fiji,

Tahiti, Ponape. Period of instruction in this curious form of cooking began about 1875 and lasted until 1928, which is now. Still going on, for once you begin you never can stop.

GUAM

FRENCH

2. California or Gold Miner Cookery, 1879 to 1889. School days.

3. New England or Cape Cod Cookery. Abode of my ancestors, 1881 to 1893.

4. Japanese, 1895 to 1898.

ITALIAN

5. Chinese, 1897 to 1899.

6. Borneo, 1896–97. One year in the jungle.

7. Chamorro or Guam Cookery, (Islas Marianas) 1898, six months. "Marooned."

8. French, 1899, 1906.

9. Capri or Near Neapolitan, 1903, six months.

10. Hudson Bay, Upper Ontario, two months. 1915.

11. Seascout Boat Cookery and Boy Scout Camps as Chief Seascout, seventeen years, and still at it. 1911 to 1928.

12. Sahara Desert, six months. Nefta! Hammamet! 1927.

13. In a cocoanut grove on the beach at Waikiki . . . to try out all these stunts to the

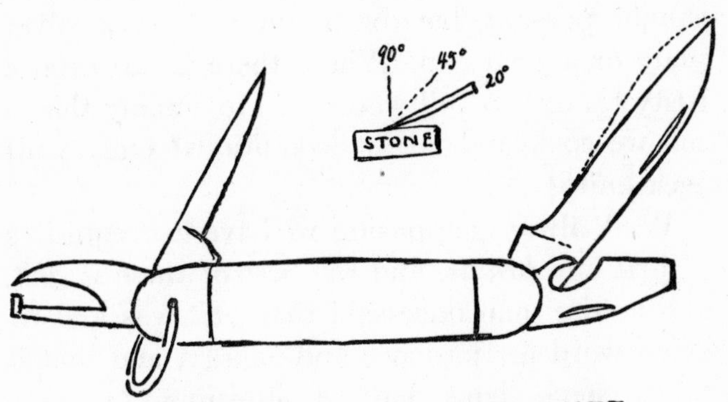

MY BATTERED OLD JACK KNIFE

scorn of the passersby, who thought I was crazy, 1928.

Do these dates overlap? Well, they did. But they represent my DIPLOMA. Now let us start cooking.

CHAPTER II

ON THE DESERT ISLAND

FOUND! A Desert Island. Here it is not possible to go back home for the salt. Here you cannot possibly borrow a gilt skewer, a silver plate or a gold cup. Where there is not even a rusty tin can to boil water in. How many things can we cook under these conditions? Only your jack-knife?

Well, always supposing we have the requisites of *grit* and *brains,* and the first of these is *grit,* and a wise man once said that *grit* was a short slang word for patience and energy, and that it takes some boys half a life-time to learn what sheer grit can accomplish . . . having the above, you can cook almost *everything.* For it is really astonishing how many good, hearty, *wise,* stick-to-your-ribs dishes can be well cooked, deliciously cooked . . . scientifically cooked . . . with only your jack-knife for a kitchen implement.

NOTE: In a later chapter we will let you have a sauce-pan, a lard-pail, a fry-pan . . . but this is strictly jack-knifery here.

THIS IS THE PLACE!

Here are some dishes: Bread, Fish, Flesh, Fowl, Vegetables, nearly all kinds, and some desserts. What more do you want?

We will begin in that Campers' Paradise, the

Desert Island where there is everything to cook and everything to cook it with (and nothing to cook it in or on). *Food,* all sorts, because this is a cook book, mostly, and not a "Young Huntsman's Manual," and *water* and *wood,* the best kind, and the will to make what you have started out to do a howling success.

Now as jack-knife cookery depends on a wisely made fire, one just big enough and hot enough to carry out your plans for a square meal with the minimum of equipment, we must discuss this highly important item:

Fire

No two fires are ever exactly alike. The sort of wood, the calories of the ground; stony, sandy,

Call this a "Corral" if you like

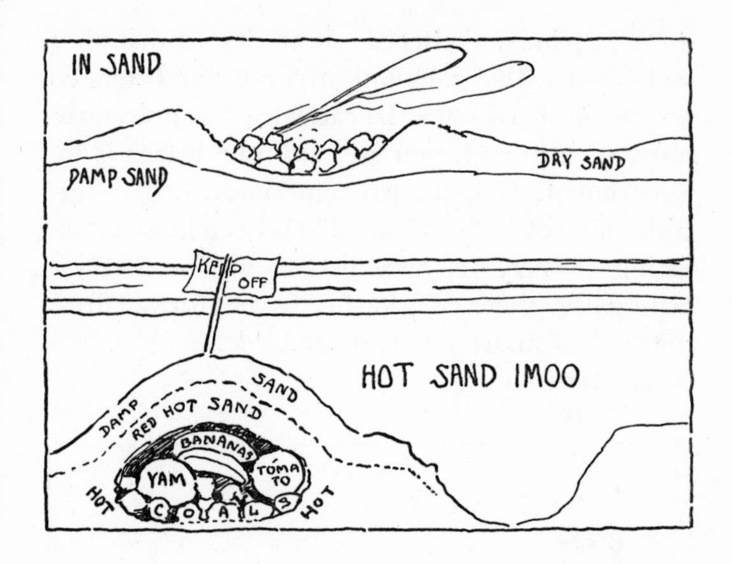
IN SAND
DAMP SAND
DRY SAND
KEEP OFF
HOT SAND IMOO
SAND
DAMP
RED HOT SAND
BANANAS
YAM
TOMA TO
HOT
COALS
HOT

CAVE.
BARK
BIG RAIN : BIGGER FIRE

muddy, windy, sheltered—bone dry or dripping wet—make the jack-knifer think and maybe scratch his head some. In each case the procedure must be different, you see, and one learns it by experiment. It is known sometimes by the biggish name of "Fire Control" and is a most interesting science. If more people practised it intelligently there would be fewer forest fires, more trees, more game, more birds.

But to resume.

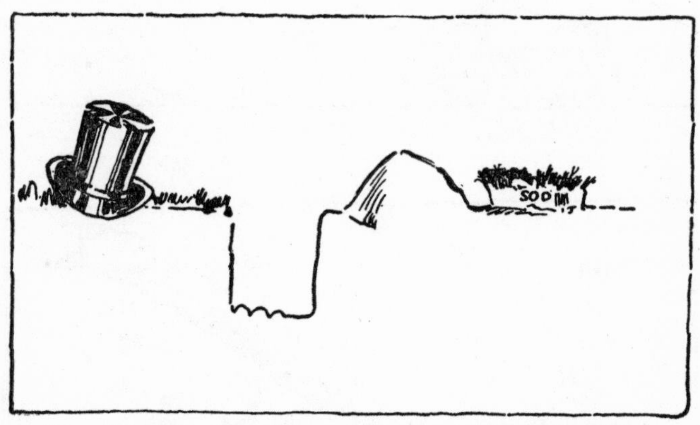

THIS WE WILL CALL "EEMOO" OR HOLE, "PLUG HAT" SIZE.

An ideal fire for one man, a cooking fire, is a small bed of bright-red hardwood coals, in a hole, or in a "corral," so that a sudden gust of wind won't scatter fire brands and destruction; one easy to extinguish by the simple method of dousing the hole full of water, or lacking that, by kicking the earth, lately scooped out, back into it.

It should be away from eddies of wind, not too near a bank, else your eyes will smart with smoke. Find a place near a comfortable stump or a grassy knoll, where, cool and collected, as a Master Jack-knifer, you may sit, watching, as from an easy chair, your breakfast, dinner, or supper coming on. Your bed of coals is best in a

TWO WAYS

scooped hollow, or a neatly dug hole called an "eemoo" but you may have to place it where you can, keeping in mind the danger that every fire wears in its smouldering heart; the stuff that may turn you into a criminal—whether you meant it or not.

The diagrams tell the story better than words.

By and by we can take up different fuels; cocoanut husks, soft wood, pine, say, or buffalo chips, peat, . . . all sorts; but for the problems now about to be tackled we have hickory charcoal, and you cannot beat that!

Kabobs and Twisters, or Meat and Bread on a Stick

Beef and Bread—the white man's mainstay, without kitchen utensils. Problems number one and number two.

When you can cook these two dishes ("dishes" is good) you belong to the great and noble order

of Jay Kays. It is not so easy. Ninety-five per cent of my "pupils" present and past, have made and do make a nasty mess of Kabobs and Twisters, so go steady and do them *right*. Right the first time, I hope, but right at last if it takes you all summer. Firstly, you are cooking a square meal for yourself alone, in quickest time, with the least bother, and then, when your time comes, as it did to Abraham Lincoln, you will be able to feed a multitude by merely multiplying the units. I mean in floods, train wrecks, cyclones and there were a lot of these this very year—perhaps the more romantic case of the wrecked yacht (this happened too) where a lot of people were wailing for food and nobody by to show them how to cook it.

First the Fire. Dig a hole as deep and big as a Plug Hat. Line it on the bottom with small stones: these hold the heat and steady your fire. Choose "non-pop" stones the size of an egg. Certain kinds explode. Look for porous, spongy-looking rocks. Geology! Start off with small dry twigs, adding larger stuff, chips from a hardwood log, then small junks of dry, hard wood to get that bed of red-hot coals before mentioned. Don't choke it—leave air spaces. You will be surprised to see how hot it will get, for it usually creates its own draft, and steadies down to a white glow, just what you want.

While this is going on you must prepare the Kabob.

Beef. By beef I mean any food like it—mutton, kidneys, goat, gazelle, moose, venison, pork. (I've never tried lizard—or snake-meat, but I hear it's wonderful.) Then there will be breasts of duck, quail, reed-birds, chicken, grouse. (I've never tried sea-gulls or buzzard and don't intend to. But you may, some day, in a tight place.)

Fresh beef! The one boy ration is about ⅓ pound. Equals two portions or helpings—one for the other fellow. For cheap and tender ask

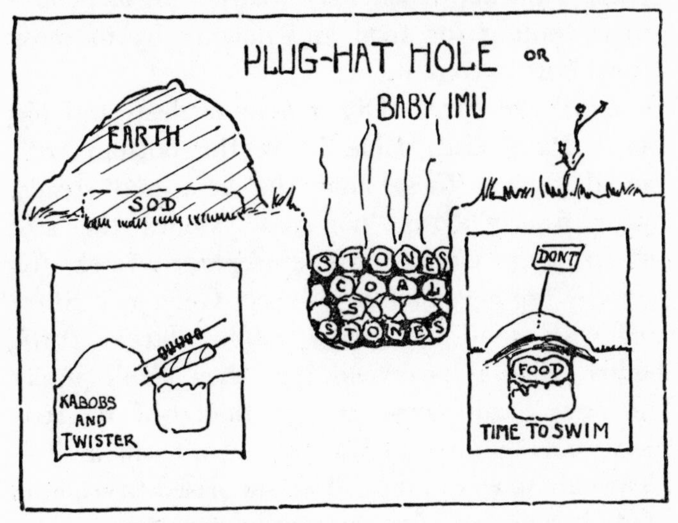

The Plug-Hat Hole, Kabobs and Twister

the butcher to sell you a skirt or flank steak. The flank has a cowl or skin over it. It keeps better with this skin on but you must strip it off before cooking. Kabobs may be made of almost anything . . . but the flank and the skirt are classical.

Your Plug-Hat Hole (my favorite method, as

you'll find out) having stopped smoking, presenting a white-hot surface of coals about the size of a soup-plate (see above diagram), you proceed as follows. Cut a green stick of some sweet wood. Taste it! Peel the bark off, leaving a wand as big around as the tip of your little finger and a foot and a half long. Sharpen both ends.

Cut your beef into pieces as big as thirty

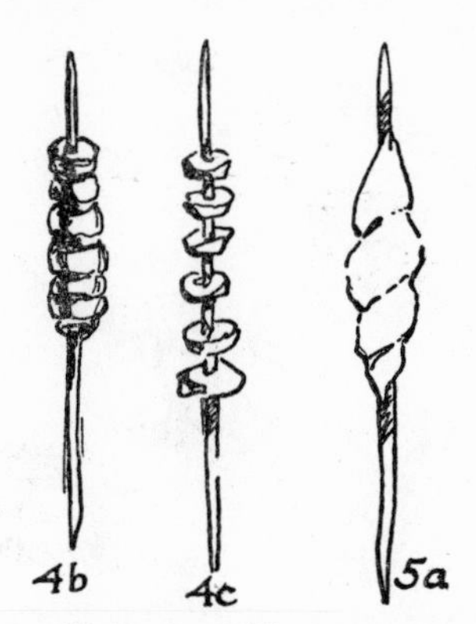

KABOBS AND TWISTER

cents. (Smaller than fifty cents and bigger than a quarter.) Spear these, string them, impale them on your stick and push them to the middle leaving a slit of daylight between each piece for *well done*—close up together for rare or "underdone." Now roll in flour, and set it aside stuck up in the ground.

When and if your fire is ready jab one end of your wand into the mound of earth that came out of the Plug Hat and let your kabob sizzle over the coals until it cooks to a lovely brown. Salt when nearly done.

This is the Persian *Kabob*—and is a sure, quick way. Kabobs may be glorified by alternating bacon, onion, parboiled (half-cooked) potatoes in between the little junks of meat. All sorts of beef, kidneys, liver, liver and bacon, kidney

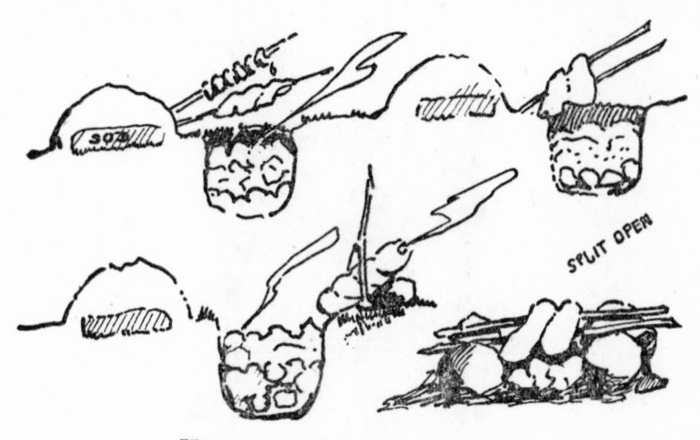

KABOB AND TWISTER "STUNTS"

and bacon, bacon, beef and onions, mutton, venison!

This is not the "Ishkibab" of the Syrians. It's an adaptation by our cousins, the British Tommies, by way of India and Egypt, of that delectable dish. The French would call it *en brochette* (brochette = little skewer). May be made on a wire but that isn't good jack-knife practice. In this same twiggy manner may be cooked Weenies (Frankfurters[1]) and small birds, chicken legs, wings, etc., also, and that wonderful invention of the Sundowners (or tramps) in Australia, the *Twister,* or bread on a stick. (Sundowners are those lean, haggard fellows that walk hundreds of miles and carry a "bush-knife" and a sack of flour. That's all they carry.)

They call this bread on a stick a ***Twister.*** It

is either a hard-tacky or "soda biscuit" sort of bread, depending on the cook. Its great virtue is *time.* It is quick work—made in a jiffy and good to eat!

NOTE: The "TWIST" is a spiral on a bigger stick, "banana" size and means work with an axe and a handy forest. Not so good.

THE TWISTER

The white man calls bread the staff of life. In a tight pinch he will abandon everything but his

[1] A friend writes: "Last week in Frankfort I tried to get some Hot Dogs. We tried 'Heisse Hunden' and 'Weenies' and at last had to give it up. They evidently do not have Frankfurters in Frankfort!"

flour, his *wheat.* Not the sickly, faded, white flour that the dudes eat, but the *whole* wheat—man's natural and best food. Man has been eating wheat for about 50,000 years and human bodies have grown used to it. One can swim a river with a bag of flour and only lose a little by wetting a thin skin of dough! Mile for mile (weight-mileage—pounds per mile) wheat is acknowledged *the* food to travel on. So every boy should know how to cook it quickly and well.

No. 1—Yarn. A South African pal told me this. A contingent of men from some big city, a platoon or so—raw troops—were given a flock of sheep and some bags of flour. Two hours later the order came to move. My friend saw men devouring half-cooked mutton with the wool still on—some men had chopped out mutton steaks, without killing the animal! As for the flour most of these non-jack-knifers had mixed it up with water, in their hats, and swallowed it, raw! When I heard this yarn years ago, it made me think. Does it make *you* think?

But to resume. Here is the Jack-Knife recipe for bread on a stick, our so-called Twister.

1. One heaping fistful of flour.
2. One five-finger pinch of Baking Powder.
3. One four-finger pinch of sugar.
4. One three-finger pinch of salt.

5. One two-finger gob of grease (fat, butter, lard, etc.).
6. One or two fistfuls of water.

NOTE: (1) Fistful: 1/2 cupful. (2) Five-finger pinch: 2/3 teaspoonful. (3) Teaspoonful. (4) 1/8 teaspoonful. (5) Size of one wad of chewing gum, or 1/2 teaspoonful.

Now, with a wooden paddle, which you will carve, on the spot, out of a piece of soft wood,

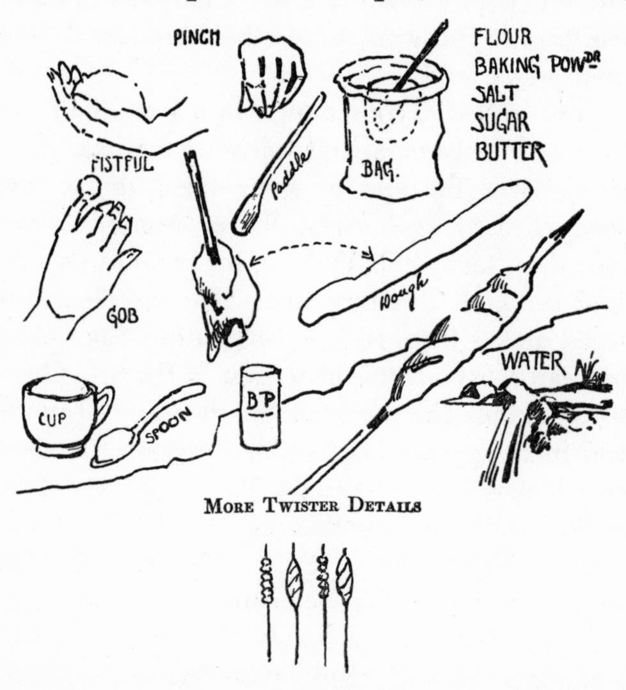

MORE TWISTER DETAILS

make a small imitation of the Plug-Hat Hole in your bag of flour. Into this little pit put your ingredients in the order named above. When you come to *grease* (No. 5) mix all up, using your hands to do this rather messy job thoroughly. Add water slowly which will, when stirred by your wooden paddle, absorb your fistful of flour and the other ingredients. The trick is to avoid lumps. Knead it well and quickly. Mix these, all dry, together at home before you start on your trip, carried in a small bank-bag or canvas bag, *if* you want to lose half the fun. If not, do it on the spot.

Now roll out your dough in a longish string, the size of a banana, and roll it on a sweet, green wood twig the size of your third finger, and sharpened at both ends. Sweet wood is determined by tasting it. Willow, for example, makes Kabobs and Twisters taste like quinine. Pine wood makes them reek of turpentine. Sometimes one can roast out this bitterness in the fire. Green wood stands the heat without burning. Jab one end in the ground so that the "twister" is about two inches from the coals. Watch it! Twist the stick round and round, until the flour puffs up and acquires a bit of crust. Then four or five inches from the fire is enough (maybe) until your twister turns a lovely *dark brown.* Now, screw out the stick. Split your twister, toast the inside, if it needs it, and there's your bread to eat with your Kabob, which has cooked at the same fire along with your "Twister."

Here are meat and bread—both deliciously cooked on a small bed of coals in a quiet corner of the cow-pasture, I mean the Desert Island. Utensils, *one knife*. Time, 30 minutes. Eat an apple for dessert—and there you are. Put out fire, fill hole, resod, and move on. How many men can do this, do you think? *Mighty few!* And the few are far between. As I said before, when you can make a good Kabob and Twister you are 95 per cent of a Jack-knifer. All the other stunts are so easy!

Sand

Sand is soft to sleep on and very romantic. "By the sad sea waves." But cooking is difficult and tents easily blow down. Keep to leeward of the ship's galley unless you like to eat sand in the stew. And in lieu of tent pegs, bury "dead men" . . . stones . . . deep in the sand to hold on to.

Bubbles

Take a pinch of B. P. and drop water on it. Bubbles! Carbonic Acid Gas is let loose. If this meeting of a Base and an Acid takes place mixed up in flour and water, dough, the imprisoned bubbles swell up and make the Dough light or spongy. Add heat and they swell bigger still. Meanwhile the heat is cooking and hardening the crust, holding in the "balloons" by the tens of thousands in what is going to be your twister. If you let these balloons burst, the dough sinks, goes flat, like punctured tires. So work fast to make a light twister.

A New Trick

Impale a frankfurter on your sweet twig. Smear it with mustard. Then wrap your twister dough around it and cook as usual. This is "wunnerful," but must be cooked to a *dark brown.*

Try sinking your Kabob, after it is *well cooked,* into your dough and then cooking it as a twister. When you pull the twig or sharpened stick out, pour a little *soy* into the hole. This is a beefsteak sandwich and a big and satisfying meal. This is known as *a la Pine Tree*—and in Flood, Cyclone, Fire and Earthquake countries

—not to forget Picnics, makes everybody happy, *if you know how.*

HER HUSBAND WAS A JACK-KNIFER

SOME OTHER WAYS OF JACK-KNIFE BREAD

When you have time you can tackle the following:

The Bannock. Create a smooth place on dry hard earth and brush it clean. On this make a fire and keep it going for at least two hours. Have a bed of coals ready, broken up fairly small by punching it down with a stone. Make a dough cake, "So big" . . . big boy, big bannock or Chupatty, as the Hindus call them. Use the Twister recipe and pat your cake to about half an inch thick. Place it gently on the hot ground, rake the coals over it and in about ten or fifteen minutes turn it over. Then test it with a smooth sharp splinter. When no dough sticks to this splinter . . . done. Eat it cold, split and toasted.

Raisins, nuts, berries—(not too many) worked

into chupatties with more sugar! Try chocolate, milk, jam—grated fresh cocoanut meat. Any odds and ends—mashed potato, mashed sweets, cooked peas, etc.

The Damper. The Chupatty on a larger scale. Here your fire must be on hard flat ground and must burn all night . . . three hours anyhow.

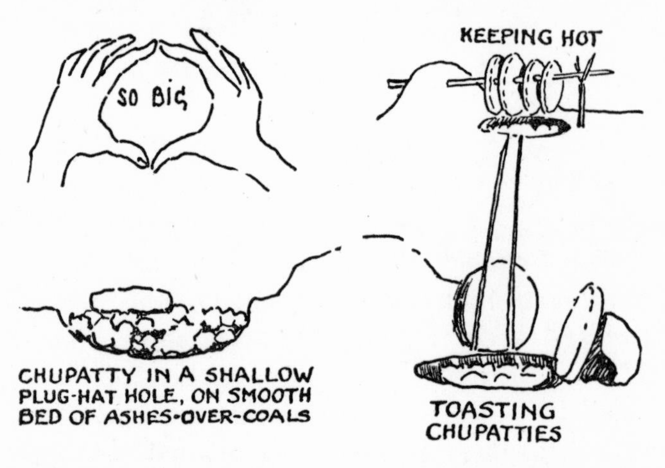

Ten pounds of flour makes a small cart wheel and will feed twenty people or more. Measured out by *Double Fistfuls,* you must count up how many pinches of Baking Powder, how much salt, how much grease . . . butter, crisco, etc., you need, which should be easy, for you had best not try a big Damper until you are very proficient with Chupatties and Twisters. Mix this on a tent flap, dust it with plenty of flour, to keep it clean, roll it up like a huge jelly roll. Carry this on your extended arm to your hot space of ground, swept clean with a long stick and a broom of leaves—sweet ones, no pine!—and as gently as

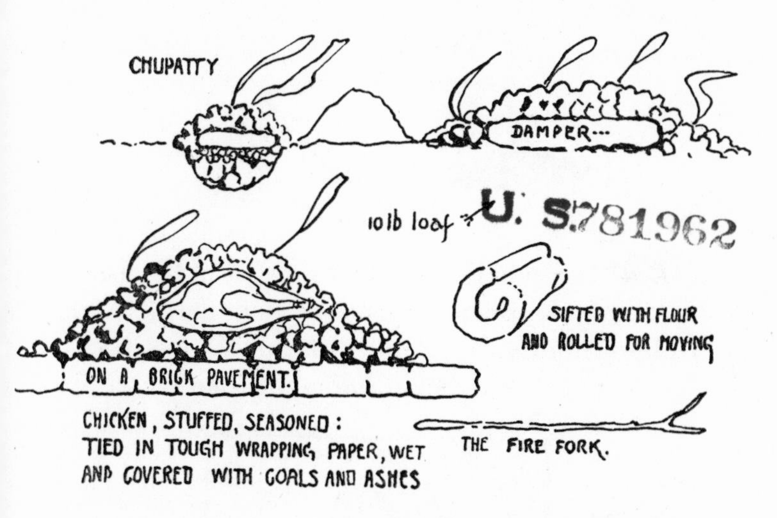

you can manage it, for shocking the dough tends to make it slump, unroll it. Then comes the hard part . . . raking the coals on top of the dough without a spade. Scrape the coals all over the top ashes and all, using a long flattened stick, for you will find it hot work, and do it as quickly as you can. The coals must be hot and close together. In about twenty minutes the puffing up process will have ceased. Now turn it over to brown the bottom. Now test it with a long sharp pointed "splinter" and if done, roll it against a tree to become cold. This is real bread and to be perfect should show no burned places. If these appear shave off the harmless carbon with your Jack-knife.

HOT SLAB

Bullets are balls of dough roasted in the ashes.

Pones are made without a pan in the Blue Ridge Mountains. A rail-splitter told me how—but I confess not having done it. The recipe is:

two-thirds corn meal to one-third white flour, an "aig," "meat drippins" (meaning bacon fat) and salt if you use butter. The aig is beaten up, the water (milk) added, and you mix this with the dry ingredients. A hot stone ready, you squeeze the pone between your palms; grease the stone and "bake" to a nice brown.

Hot holes in the ground, hot slabs of stone, hot coals—these are the primitive methods of cooking without pots or pans. But there is another already suggested by what I call the Plug-Hat Hole. The Imu of Polynesia.

The Imu (Pronounced EEMOO) or Prehistoric "Plug-hat Hole"

This was an invention of the stone age man, and a very ancient method of Jack-knifery. You heat stones in a hole in the earth, put your food, meat or vegetables, into it and cover it over with leaves and earth. In this way you may cook one spud or a sixty-pound hog, smothered in yams, bananas and . . . anything, nearly, and take it out an hour or so later to find everything cooked to a nicety. Anybody can do it!

There are many varieties of the Imu. Clam bakes, Bean Holes, Deep Imus, and Shallow Imus. They tell me that the age-long scars of Imus or OOmoos (Mongolian way of saying it) show a migration of Ground-cooking Jack-knifers from the Mediterranean clear across Mesopotamia into Afghanistan, Siberia, Northern and Southern Japan—thence from island to island, two or three thousand miles across the

Pacific Ocean, to Hina, the Polynesian Atlantis, a huge continent that slowly sank into the sea, leaving the colonies stranded outside: Hawaii, pronounced Ha-WAH-ee, Marquesas, Tahiti, Samoa, New Zealand, Tonga, Fiji and so on. All agree that the Imu is the last word in Jack-knifery so here is the way to do it.

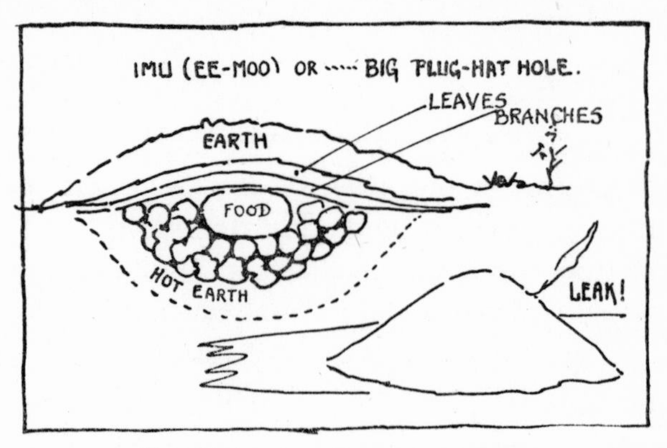

THIS SHOWS THE THEORY OF IMU'S

Incidentally I once assisted in feeding two hundred hungry people from one immense imu at Halawa, Molokai, Hawah-ee. Then, later, I fed sixty or more Columbia teachers in an imu at Bear Mountain, on the Hudson River, New York State. They staged a wonderful funereal Hula at the grave and beautiful naiads and brave warriors vied with each other in maiden grace and manly vigor, crowned with chaplets and garlands of flowers. When the fifty-pound pig was uncovered, cooked to a T, a mighty shout went up. They didn't leave as much as a trotter. No cookery can beat the imu, they all averred.

It is an *emergency trick*. Much easier than cooking a pig in a stove, I do declare! Learn it, boys, get ready for the day when you are wanted to step into the breach. Your time will surely come.

Begin with one big potato. Line the bottom of a hole in the ground as big and as deep as a plug hat—or larger, with stones. Pile the earth that comes out of this hole on the windward rim, see page 24. If you have taken up a sod pile the earth a-top of it so you may **RESOD** the scar in the grass when you move on. Make a smart fire on the stones, at the bottom, of some light inflammable stuff, feeding it with charcoal or short junks of hard wood until your fire pit is red hot. If the ground is damp a few stones on top will help—in this case stones as large as a golf ball, porous, igneous stones that are not liable to burst with the heat. This is Geology!

When this fire is well under way look about for something to cover your hole and have it ready. Twigs with the leaves on, short pieces of green stick (for rafters, in fact) on which you are going to pile earth. Now, when the smoke has died down and the small stones, very hot, have settled down some, drop in Mister Spud and *immediately* begin rigging your rafters. Cover with the largest leaves, "sweet" rather than bitter or resinous for the latter will taint your food, of course, and then pile dirt on top, beginning at the sides. Work fast to avoid having your roof burst into flames. Pat the earth gently into a

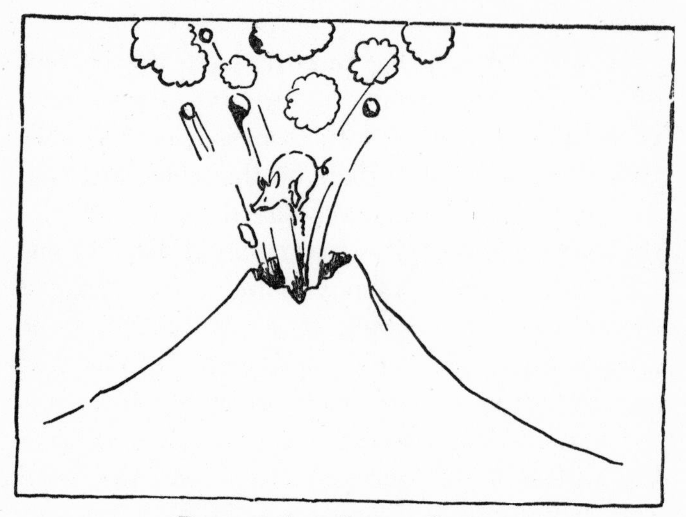

POPPABLES! OR APPLIED GEOLOGY

mound about two inches deep. Allow no leaks, which are betrayed by smoke.

Then go and tend to other business.

Now comes the hard part: when is your big potato done? Well, forty-five minutes to an hour and a half, depending on the stored-up heat in this "fire-less" cooker. Under average conditions say one hour, but never more than twenty-four. Your "cooker" is cooling all the while, you see. Here begins the good guessing that makes the good "Imu" or "Plug-hat-holer" like a good physician . . . he must learn by experience to guess right. My old Hawaiian "male nurse," or Kahu (Tutor) said "Better half burned than half cooked" and somehow his pigs, chickens, vegetables were always deliciously done. But he had cooked for my late sovereign, Lunalilo I, King of the Sandwich Islands, and was a past master.

Old Kawika. His Portrait

The Imu being of suitable size for what you want to cook and the heat adequate . . . you might allow 20 minutes over the first hour for every 10 lbs. over twenty-five of food, and the Imu should be, roughly, three times the diameter of your pile of food.

To cook a full-sized sheep, skinned and cleaned, would require an Imu five feet across and three layers of hot stones the size of half a brick. Give it one and one-half hours. In the case of a large hog, the inner parts must be well cooked by thrusting suitably sized red-hot stones under the hams, gashed to take them, snugly,

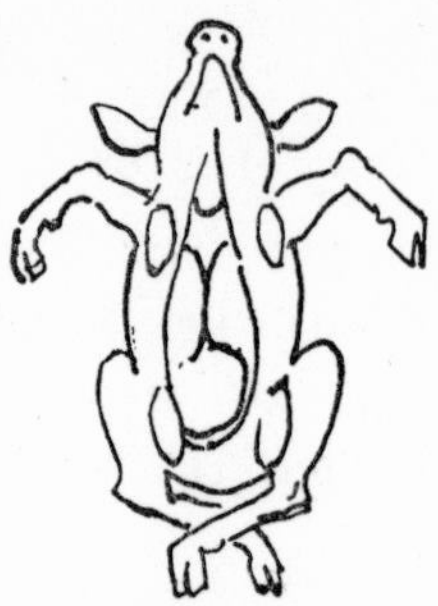

HOT STONES INSIDE

into the throat and into the open belly. Then truss the hog up by the legs, and on a bed of sweet leaves, with cover of the same, lay over him (where he lies surrounded by sweet potatoes,

READY FOR THE IMU

half-ripe bananas, corn on the cob, chickens tied up in leaves, tied-up bundles of greens [for spinach] and so forth) brush, green hay, sea weed, clean flour sacks, canvas, mats, . . . but for Jack-knifers . . . just leaves or hay must do, and then, for this is on a bigger scale than the small and deeper Plug-Hat Hole, about four to five inches of loose earth, which you need not pat down in this case.

The Imu or eemoo is good for bushels of food: great fat swine, whole sheep, crates of chickens and turkeys, pecks of vegetables . . . or one little broiler, a quail or a plover. You simply learn by experiment and common "horse sense" . . . beginning with one large potato and *working up*.

The smallest game birds are cooked by shoving a hot stone into their cleaned out insides and toasting them a little on the coals, but you may trifle with all sorts of things to see what suits this style of cookery best. For my part I do not care for beef cooked under ground . . . it seems to absorb flavors from the earth. Pigs and sheep —ah! good!!

Cover is frequently impossible to find . . . no cover, no imu. In the Southern States and North, too, we found wild grape leaves quite good enough to cover and wrap food for the Imu. In the Pacific we have the Ki and the Banana growing far and wide . . . with immense leaves, a foot wide, some of them, and a characteristic flavor. But Butcher paper, wet and tough, has been made to do. In a pinch, napkins, towels, cheese cloth, carpet, canvas . . . .

To handle hot stones use a staff and forked

stick as in the diagram. Dipping the hands into cold water you may pick up a hot stone and toss it about . . . as the Kanakas do. That takes nerve.

Try a dozen plug hats and see what happens. You will improve steadily.

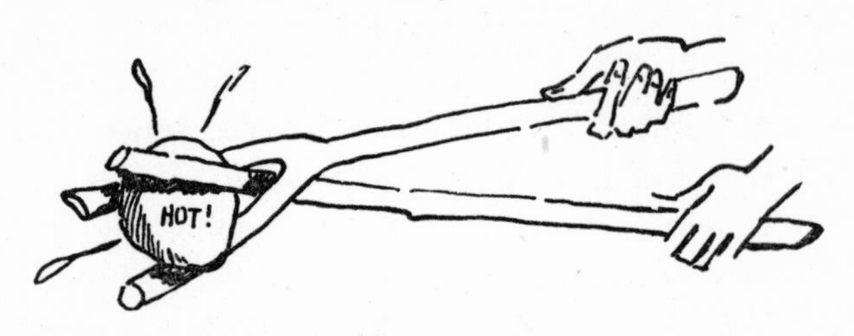

Why not chuck your spuds in the ashes? As the man said who sold a "sure death to cockroaches" consisting of two blocks of wood between which you put the roach and squeezed—When asked "Why not step on 'em?" he answered "Well,—that's a good way too!"

In the ashes! Try hot pebbles—then the spuds come out clean and you can eat them skin and all. The vitamines (food kick) is in the skins! Delicious! But you can't beat imued[1] sweets, spuds (with salt in a tiny hole which you cut out with your knife and then plug up), bananas (great!); tomatoes (wrapped, salted); apples (sugared)—oh, well, almost anything!

Clam Bake. For one man! Plug-hat Hole,

[1] Imu (Imm-oo) is the hole. *Kalua* is the act of cooking in an Imu—but that's too, too highbrow. Pass!

Red hot—line with a mess of seaweed, then clams (oysters, lobster, etc.), more seaweed, but no earth. Not necessary, and—Don't cook more'n you can eat!

Bean hole—doesn't belong here. See *Beans.*

Sand Hole. Few people will believe what hot sand can do! Sand Imu is simply red hot *dry sand:* bury your food *well wrapped* (in the case of potatoes, bananas and other thick-skinned fruits they go in naked) and then cover with about three inches of *damp* (not wet) sand. Put a flag up or somebody will surely step on it. One hour (go and swim), dig sand away from one side: there is a "cave-in," and—your deliciously cooked stuff is left high and—luscious. The salt water steam does it! A noted author, Harry Leon Wilson, on tasting my sand-cooked sweets said—"That's the way to cook 'em!" The sand must be *very* dry. You spread the fire over the sand (a fire of driftwood?) then, when your wrapped food is in the ashes, scrape the hot sand into a mound over the hole; as I said before, *Work quickly*—dig down to the damp sand on one side and make a dome or roof, an inch or two thick, all over the hot top. Now pat it gently, set up a signal—and—go and swim. In an hour your food will be cooked and kept warm for hours after.

Your third trial ought to be a success!

(See the diagram on page 19.)

THE WHACKING BIG CHEROOT

There are dozens of wild plants that boil down into good, healthy spinach. Dandelion; pig-weed, sweet potato vine; squash flowers, mix any of the above. Almost anything that rabbits will eat *is liable* to make spinach, but some are bitter, some poisonous. Know your Botany! But how, with no lard-tin? No pot—no billy—no can? In New England the only leaves suitable are wild grape

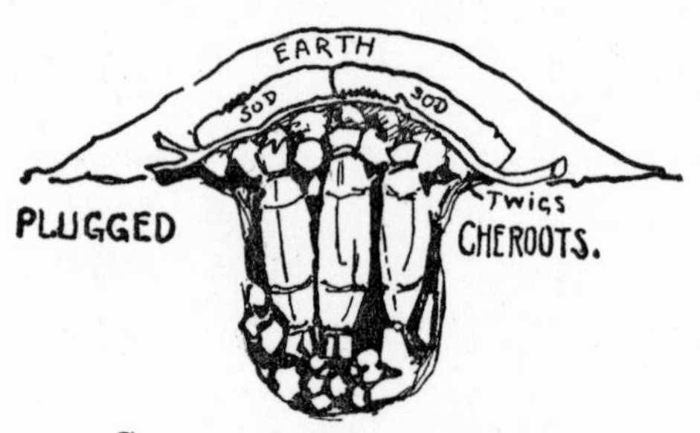

CHEROOTS IMU-ED, OR "PLUGGED"

leaves, or corn husks, ditto down South—but in the Tropics you can use *Kee* (Dracaena) or banana leaves or *Hau*—failing all else and *starving,* tear up your undershirt. Wrap your greens into a thick cigar—size of your wrist—and tie up with green leaves and bark very snug. (Don't forget the salt.) Pack this in your Plug-hat Hole (which must be deep and oblong and mighty hot) clap on your big sod, etc., supported by twigs, and—wait a while. Soft, squidgy stuff takes half an hour (maybe) but tough spinachy stuff takes longer, an hour perhaps.

Oh, how good a mess of sloozy, hot spinach tastes when you are dead beat! Next to stir-a-bout (See Stir-about, below.) this is a prime reviver for an utterly exhausted man or boy! You eat it, of course, with a smooth chip or a paddle-spoon or an oyster shell. Don't think you can "pull this off" the first time, either. You must try all these stunts near home. Get Ready! Your time may come! Who knows when?[1]

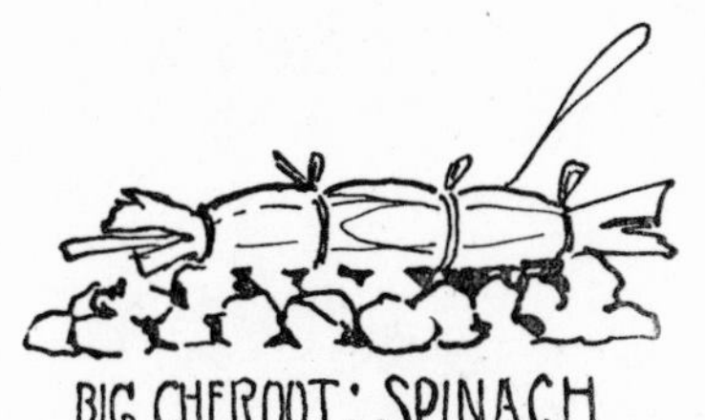

Note: "Stirabout" is thin flour and water cooked a few minutes with a pinch of salt. It hits the spot for the down and outers—but as it calls for a cup or sauce-pan, is not strict Jack-Knifing!

Fish in Leaves. First catch your fish. Clean, wash, salt. Wrap snugly in green leaves, tie up with bark, and toast on the coals.

Fish in clay, fish in moss, fish planked, fish

[1] I once successfully saved a pal's life (so he said at the time) by wrapping taro-tops (same as the mainland Jack-in-the pulpit, botanically—Indian Root! said to be poison, so don't try it!) in Ki (Kee) leaves and roasting the cheroots on hot coals. Great! See *Fish* for the same trick (p. 49).

stuffed with bread and herbs and baked in a clay oven, fish cut into neat junks, rolled in egg and bread crumbs, then dropped into deep and very hot fat (when you have a pail) even fish

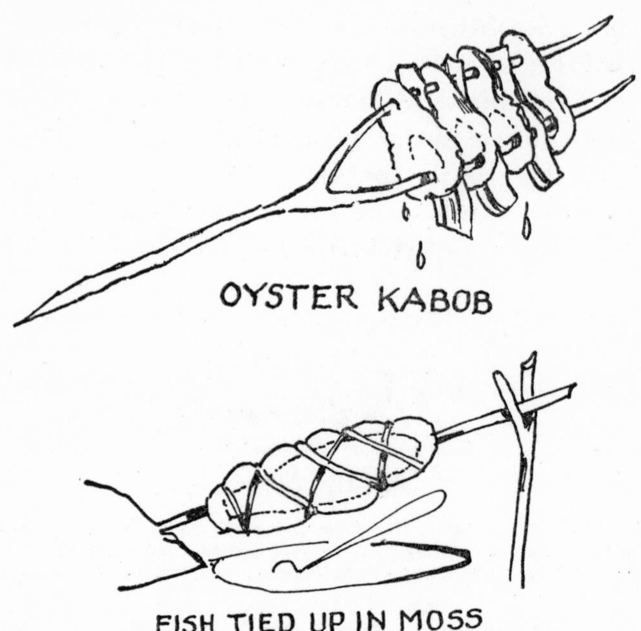

KABOBBED with bacon strips between . . . there is a whole book of dodges for you. In this book are most of them. Try the rest yourself. Instead of bread crumbs you may dip things in cream of wheat. Then fry deep.

There are other ways of Jack-knifing a meal.

SOME OF A JACK-KNIFER'S DODGES

CHOPS À LA TWIG

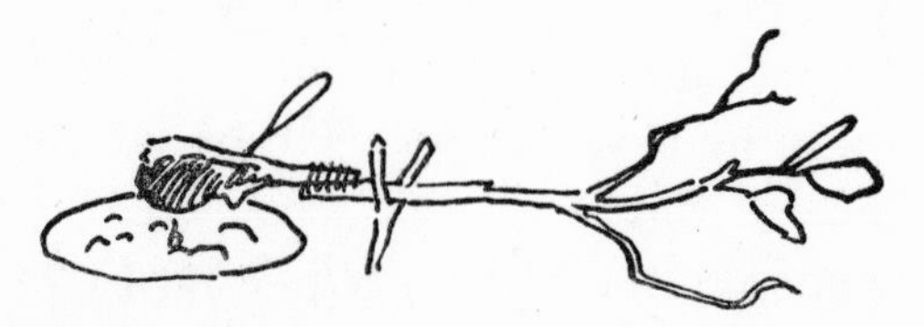

BALANCE THE CHOP, ETC., WITH THE LEAFY END

THE CAVE-OVEN

The cave explains itself by the diagram below where you see the over-door-stone heating in the chimney flue. This works!

Lots of fun. At Murray Bay, Canada, we made and cooked a raisin cake in a bark dish, in a cave-oven and the girls, six of 'em, squealed with delight. Technique: You dig, with your pick and shovel (stick and hands) into a *clay* bank; get

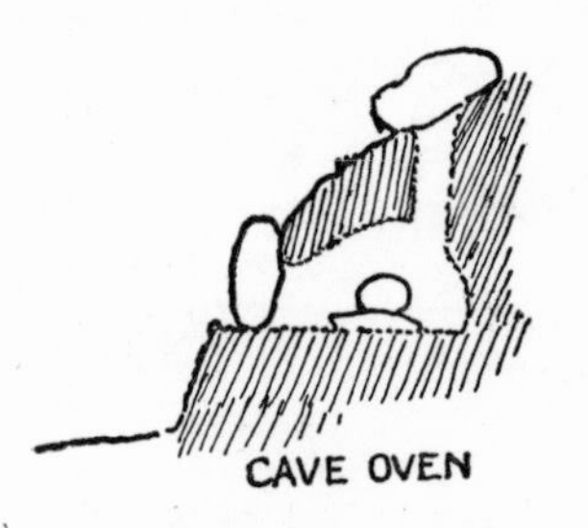

CAVE OVEN

it hot with very dry, light, twiggy-snappy wood. Then you rake the floor of your oven clean (work quick) carefully put your cake (dough, spuds, etc.) away in, close the hole with a flat stone also heated (see diagram) and *wait*. Give it *undisturbed* 20 minutes—then *peek*. Your first experiment may be—(1) Only dough; (2) Only a lump of blackened flour; (3) A beautifully cooked loaf of cake, bread, duck (see Stuffing) or some such thing.

Remember: A few ashes are *not* poison.

NOTE: Stuffing: wet stale bread, chopped apple, onion, butter, salt and pepper: sage, thyme, marjoram and rosemary: pinches only.

FOR A LONG STAY: CLAY OVEN

Make a frame (wicki-up) of switches or finger-big withes. Braid in, or tie in, grass or hay or leaves. Then plaster with not too soft clay or mud, then burn out.

Bakes bread!

HOT SLAB

Chops, steaks, weenies,—kidneys, broilers, squabs, rabbits, hares—all grill to perfection on a *flat hot stone,* if the stone is just hot enough!

See page 49 for a "hot slab."

I'm sorry to be vulgar here, but it can't be helped. There is a device known as the Spit Thermometer. *You wet your finger* and touch the stone with it. If it goes "spizzzz" it's not hot enough: if it "pops" it is *too* hot. When it goes "spit" it is just right.

Why bother with all these when a bed of coals will do it *better?* Answer: just for fun. "Adventures" in applied physics and chemistry. To keep you out of mischief.

Besides, different method, different flavor!

Steak or Chops

This is the Jack-knife method for cooking a large steak, chops, ham, etc., and it beats all the French, Italian and Dutch Blue Ribbon ways *hollow*. One is usually very hollow when he does it. That may be the secret.

Listen, boy! Have your Plug-hat Hole under way for spuds, corn, bananas. Have your dinner table on the grass cleared of rubbish; your bark plates ready, your two-pronged forks nicely sharpened. Fifteen minutes before you "wehe ka papale" (take off the hat) of your baby Imu, fan (with your hat, of course) all the ashes, white as snow, off a bed of coals *twice the size of your steak.*

Don't puncture your steak, drop it gently on one side of the bed-o-coals. Leave it about one minute. With your paddle or tongs turn it over to a fresh place and let it rest there. Salt the top here. Wait until the singing begins—five minutes about. Fan (away from the steak) the now again hot first bed-o-coals. Turn the steak back another five minutes. Salt. Stand by the baby Imu, or the Plug-hat Hole. Turn out your roasted corn, your steamed-roasted potatoes. Call all hands!

Serve. To be really smart, use charcoal in hunks as big as a golf ball and red to the core. They fall off! Smaller bits are apt to stick to the beef. Anyhow *'tain't poison!* Notice these pitfalls and keep clear. The bigger the steak, bigger and deeper must be the bed-o-coals. Better under-done (rare) than "cooked to death" for you can put it back in the first instance. Time this just right, "your time will come" and some day win lasting renown.

THIS BEATS A HAT OR A LEAF!

You begin to see now, I hope, that it is not the Jack-knife that helps one out of a scrape but the boy who wields it. Only a Jack-knife seems rather pathetic unless you have educated yourself to use it. I frequently ask boys to show me theirs and some of them produce a weak, spindly pen-knife that was given them for Christmas

"With best love from Aunt Jane." With it you might cut a watermelon, but I doubt it. Others produce a "Toadstabber" so nicked, bruised and dull that an hour at the grindstone would scarcely fit it to cut soap.

Our American Jack-knife! If I had my way, no Yank, Dixie, or Native Son would be allowed to even *whistle* the Star Spangled Banner who carries no Jack-knife.

A real one. Not too long a blade, but of good steel and kept as sharp as a razor. This book is not for babies, so sharp and strong is the word.

(See the Knife on page 15.)

This is the kind I recommend, actual size. You can get it from the Boy Scout Supply Department in any large town or city.

A larger, heavier knife is called a Bowie, kreiss, cane-knife, machete, parang, cutlass or dirk. This dirk takes the place of the much more dangerous hatchet and axe . . . but it cannot take the place of these in big, man-sized work, as in building a log cabin or in clearing land. The dirk is good for all a boy wants, going light. It will lop off a hardwood branch with one blow and bring down a dead tree in time. It seldom *misses.* It hates to glance and is in consequence safer than a small axe. It is easy to carry. It stays sharp a long time if deftly handled. It is worn on the belt, or tucked into your pack, of which more later on, is sheathed in a handsome manner and always tied in on the march or climbing.

The dirk is so useful that I will start a new angle in "Emergency" Cooking for Boys, and we will branch out into some things not exactly regulation Jack-knifery. We will adopt a few more tools, the dirk, the pot and the pan. The cup can wait. For the present you must drink out of your hand.

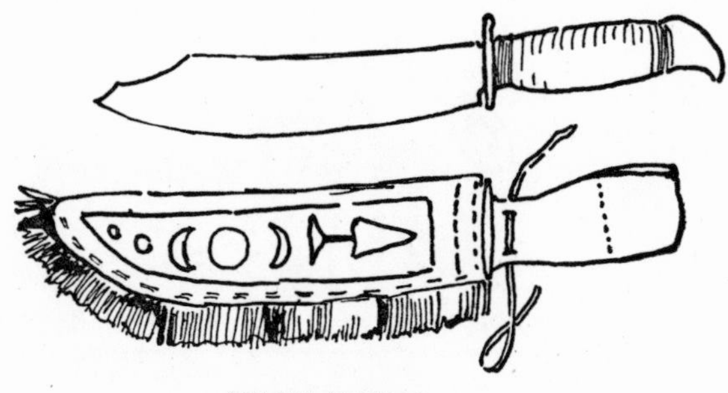

THE DIRK

But we must keep our jack-knives strong and sharp against the day when we find ourselves minus this added "High-brow" machinery. The more tools the less brains needed.

We are about to enter the adventure land of Stews, Baked Beans, Rice and Chowders.

A Jack-Knife *Stew* is done by the Afghans. They pack a cleaned sheep's stomach with pieces of mutton and vegetables, season with salt, etc., and then, neatly tied up, they imu it in the ground.

However, we must now describe some non-Jay Kay articles. Too bad, you'll say!

GOING LIGHT

The dirk. Made by the village blacksmith from a worn hasp. Ten to fifteen inches long. Study the diagram. At "A" is the part used as an axe.

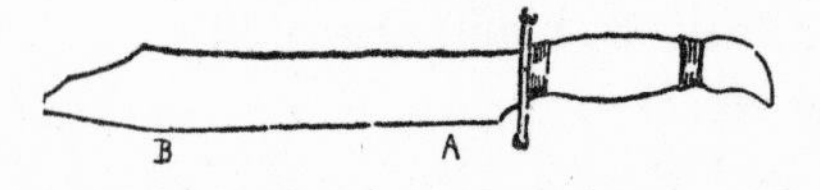

At "B" you keep it as sharp as a razor for skinning game, butchery, shaping big stuff like canoe paddles, camp furniture—whittling, slicing, etc.

The pot. The cheapest is the lard pail and all boiled or simmered things can be done in it to perfection. But you may develop fine technique in a tomato can. If you can manage the Boy Scout Cook-Kit, with nested pail, plate, fry pan, knife, fork, spoon . . . all in a case with strap, well and good. The pan is the top or lid of the lard pail and in it you fry potatoes, but I confess it makes a very wobbly pan. You can fry potatoes in the deep pail . . . that is handier.

Here you have the cheapest cook kit on the market. They come free. You cannot beat that . . . for cost.

A real Cook Kit is better, but costs money. Leave it at that!

Rigging the Pail, or Billy or Pot

In the accompanying diagrams you see some ways of rigging the Pail.

(1) *Rocky.* Same as Corral. This is where you cannot dig a hole. Pail is swung on a notched stick called a Trammel. Pail is lifted or lowered by manipulating the supports.

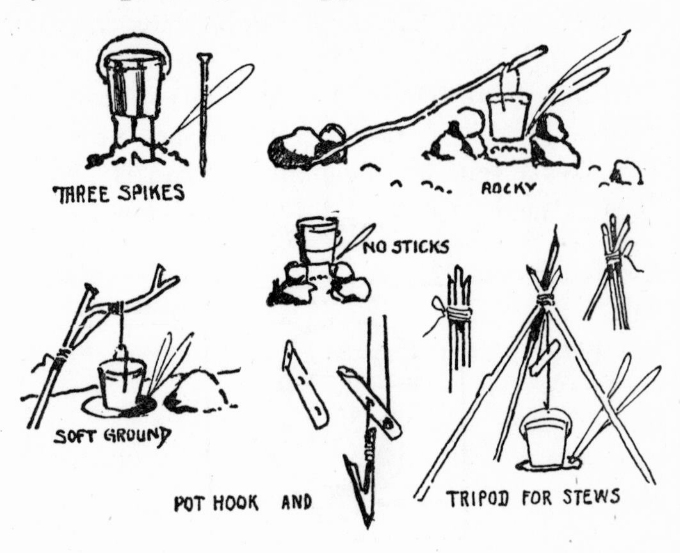

(2) *Tripod.* Handy for stew and safer than No. 1. Over a Plug Hole stew will "simmer" (boil very gently) for *four hours,* without adding fuel. The stones and *good* charcoal do it. Your "pot-hook" is a piece of wire on a string. Fashion a "slide" and be able to regulate your heat to a nicety. Point your tripods so they will hold the ground.

(3) *Soft ground.* Simple. Hang the pail first —then scoop your hole just where you want it—

under the pail. Remove pail. Build fire. Put pail back.

(4) *No lumber.* "Sticks" seldom handy except from living trees. (Not fair cutting a living tree.)

(5) *Three Bridge-Spikes.* Very handy indeed where there are no stones and no sticks. Hammer them down with your Dirk handle. *Then* build your small fire. As fire burns low and cools off, drive nails deeper. See?

(6) *The Classic Bean Hole!* We will never forget, my pal Hank and I, our experiments with beans for *100 people.* We tried them first in an enormous iron pot, "soak a night, boil till half soft, bake a night." The first bushel of beans, when soaked, overflowed, all over the place—the drill ground of the old Armory in Honolulu. So we divided the lot, boiled them in two huge pots, dug holes and baked them a night. A high wind blew up that morning and the too thin covering of earth blew off. Our coals, which should have been *damped off,* began to glow and—the beans—buckets of beans—were hopelessly burned. I must tell you here that *all out-door cookery* is a series of good guesses—that's why it's the sporting-est sort of fun. We buried these million beans, and *tried it again.* "If at first you don't succeed, try, try, try again." The second experimental batch was a

howling success. So two weeks later we soaked, boiled, and baked enough beans to feed Pharaoh's Army—gathered 200 hungry boys, invited a distinguished personage to inspect the show. He arrived glittering, with his resplendent staff, while we, trembling at the honor accorded us, led him smiling to the great Bean arena. Darn it, he took a shortcut and went to his knees in a filthy puddle of two-weeks' old beans! While the staff were scraping his leggins I looked at Hank. He was as white as paper—so was I. We both saw Leavenworth Military Prison and ten years hard labor—written in the sky, while those unmannerly kids, losing all morale, cheered and whistled. But that grand old sport just laughed; ate a plateful of our *good* beans (standing) and made us a bully speech besides. I heard him, however, give the order to his driver: "Home, *Corporal, quick!*"

Beans. Lard pail beans are soaked over night and then boiled till the skin puckers. Rig carefully, watch them and add water if necessary. Then for two fistfuls of cleaned and picked beans, add salt, a five-finger-pinch (See *Handy Scale,* page 163) of brown sugar or "some molasses," and a clove of garlic, if you like it. Put a hunk of salt pork near the top. Sometimes you may add a tomato and an onion cut fine. Then you must see to it that a little water shows at the top. Put the "pan" top on and bury it in your Plug-hat Hole, stone-lined, good and hot. Cover the whole pail with coals and ashes—then earth. Allow no leaks. Next morning, or noon, or at dinner, dig 'em up, and "let Nature take its course." Some of us can stand beans nearly every day.

For high wind use an Imu or Plug-hat Hole. In dead calm or sheltered nook, on hard or *wet ground* (in which all Imu-s and P.-H. H.'s are *impossible*) use the stone platform and piled-up coals and ashes below.

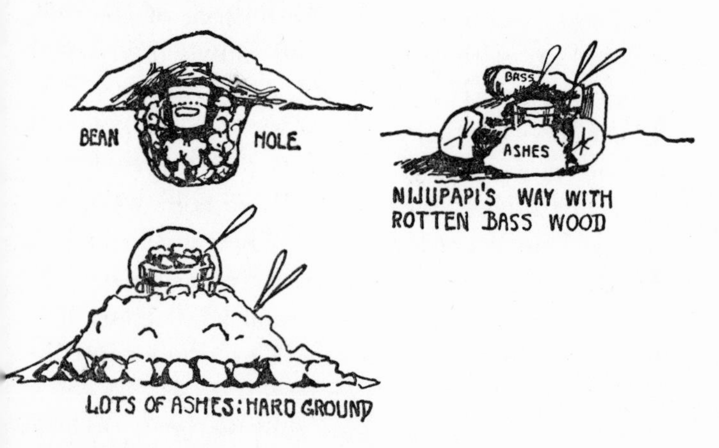

In a gentle breeze (wet ground or strong or hard—too hard to dig into) use old and rotten wood, very dry, such as Bass Wood, which smoulders—or Hau or Wiliwili in the Pacific—or anything that burns slowly: Buffalo Chips, say. Try out various things—what will burn slowly so as not to burn the beans.

Mixing ashes and dust with red hot coals makes them burn slower—but open air bean-holes must be *watched,* and that calls for "time off the fun." You must make Nature do the work.

Nijupapi is one of my Indian names—and Peter of Hudson Bay called me that; and would go a mile for rotten Bass-wood for his "open-air" bean-hole.

Cocoa. Mix two teaspoons of cocoa and sugar in a teaspoon of Klim in the bottom of the pail. Stir it up with water added slowly and let it come to a boil. It should cook a few minutes only. This makes a cup.

Coffee. Half a fistful of coffee for each boy . . . big husky ones only. Pour cold water on this and let it stand a while. Then put your pail (Billy, coffee-pot, tin cup, tomato can or fry-pan) on a hot bed of coals and let it come to a boil. Then let it just *not* boil, or simmer, on the edge of the P.-H. H., or bed of coals. To settle the grounds pour in some cold water or drop in some spotlessly clean gravel from the brook that has been boiled and cooled off. Or a crushed egg shell. Or set it on the ground to clear. Or drink it Turkish Style, grounds and all.

Stews

Stew is very popular on a desert island, or one-night camp. It can cook (on a tripod, usually) all night, rigged high while your coals are hot, and lowered when they have died down. Only a little heat from the Plug-hat Hole is sufficient but it must continue for two or three hours. When your coals are nearly gone, add a chunk of green wood and see that the water does not boil away.

There are all kinds of *stews*. Chicken, duck, beef, mutton. When you put everything in sight into your pot you'll get Hunters' stew, or Brunswick stew, or Burgoo—but the main thing is SLOW COOKING. As I said before *put good things in*—and there they will be when your stew is done unless you *burn it* or the string catches fire or somebody kicks over the tripod. Stews are risky for this reason—but—mighty good to eat with a flap-jack or a chupatty.

The usual proportions are two-thirds meat (or game) to one-third green stuff—potatoes, onions, carrots, tomatoes and some herbs, a little parsley, a bay leaf, a sprig of rosemary, basil, marjoram, green ginger, garlic—only pinches of course. Just enough to *recognize* the added flavor. Some of my stews have been likened to warm hair tonic so go slow on condiments. Being a *white Kanaka,* I like chili and curry-powder (a very little) in mine. In duck stew some chopped olives and a dash of soy!

Having started your plug-hat and rigged your pot or pail we will make that old stand-by, ***Irish stew.*** (Later on we can tackle "Exeter Stew" and "Scotch Stew" Bouillabaisse (Fish Stew), Oyster Stew, Lobster Stew—but if you can make good Irish Stew, the rest are easy. It is largely a question of ***Fire Control.*** (By this time you begin to see what I mean by that!) Irish Stew is mutton stew. Beef Stew is "Exeter Stew" with a little vinegar and dumplings. Duck stew is "Salami"—and so on.

Irish or Mutton Stew

The *usual* proportion is 2/3 mutton to 1/3 vegetables—or for one boy ½ pound of mutton to (about) two ounces (⅛ lb.) of vegetables—but the proportion may vary to our easy-to-remember, fifty-fifty, or half and half. Occasionally your stew will be *all* mutton—with some flour to thicken it (not bad) but that would be a "Stewed Mutton."

Start your fire in a convenient place—*sheltered* for stews—and rig your tripod and pot-hook *or* trammel. Tripod works best, I find. Break out your mutton, onion, potato, parsley salt-and-water. Cut your mutton, and cut off some of the fat, as big as "fifty-cents." Wash, pare and slice your potato (or potatoes) and your onion and carrots, leaving two fairly handsome junks of potato aside, and a couple of seed or "button" onions.

Put slices of potato in the bottom of your pail or pot. Then pieces of mutton, then onions and so on, until all ration is used. Cover with water, add parsley (just a pinch) and let it boil up, once, then skim it.[1] You now rig for a long slow *simmer*—for the very edge of boiling—and cook one hour and a half to two hours—*or* until the mutton is tender and the potatoes have begun to dissolve. Forty minutes before this drop in your saved-out potatoes and onions to give the stew "style." Cover your pot—and *cook slow;* once again *Cook Slowly.*

You may do the above with beef (brisket is cheap) and add a soup-spoonful of vinegar and flour-balls or *dumplings* (made by mixing chopped suet or beef fat, parsley, salt, etc. (some other herb too, if you have it) with your "twister dough" rolling it into golf balls and adding them forty minutes before your stew is done. This is the ancient British "Exeter Stew" or nearly it!

[1] In cooking in a big pot, a wash-boiler for instance, the cook must *skim* until all scum disappears. See Wash boiler cookery, page 150.

Mighty good, anyhow. Eat the above with a toasted chupatty and "Praise God from Whom all blessings flow."

Cold chicken, left over morsels, almost anything stews up. A few beans, peas, raisins, rice —all help to swell out a stew—even *bread crumbs!*

To thicken a no-potato stew proceed to make a white or brown *sauce.* Use your bacon fat. Any sort of drippings, or grease—heat this (a tablespoonful) and scatter 50-50 flour into it. Stir it about until it is a golden brown. Then add hot water from your too thin stew and *stir.* This stuff must always cook a while.

Yarn. When I was about twelve-years old, *ice cream* was so rare a treat (in old Honolulu) that only the King could have it—(ice was so hard to get and *keep*). When, one day, a huge chunk was left in the road by the careless ice-man—it slid off his cart I suppose, we boys pounced on it with yells. We dragged this cake of fast-melting ice to the kitchen-house and the cook being asleep I volunteered to make *ice cream.* I was hailed as a hero! I mixed a sort of a batter with milk and corn starch, put in some sugar, and we all took turns freezing it. Salt and pounded ice —easy. *But I hadn't cooked the mixture.* My four pals and I, for once, had all the "ice cream" we could eat. We then retired, to digest our fulsome meal, under the old monkey-pod tree. Johnnie was the first to have a sort of convulsion. He rolled around and yelled "I'm poisoned" and then Willie and Arthur and Ephie—all had spasms. I was spared, somehow. After a short, dazed rest from their spasmodic exercises—(the grass was white with milk)—my stricken chums started to go home. I felt like the Ancient Mariner with the albatross on my neck—for these pale, drawn faces turned balefully on me, the author of their woe. They were just going limply out the gate—when all three turned back and ran up with yells of glee to watch me "throw up my commission" as they say in the army. I had been spared—*but not for long.*

Be sure and cook your flour!

Farther on we will show you how to make sauce—*thickening;* both White and Brown.

Hurry-up Stew

Like these other stews but you proceed thus: Boil your vegetables in unsalted water on a brisk heat. You need not wait for *coals*—get going. Cover with water. Potatoes, cut small, boil in 20 to 30 minutes. Put on to boil. Onions take one hour. Use your head now: fry the onions and the meat in your fry-pan, if you have one (top of your lard-pail, if not) in grease. Then in the same pan *sear* or nearly cook your meat or mutton. When the onions are yellow brown and the meat tender put all in the pail. Your stew will be done under an hour. This is fast for stew—don't forget salt and seasoning. We might as well have it good!

TABLE SET!

When you make a stew you have time to make a chupatty, toast it, put on your cocoa, get out your pat of butter, place it, cool from the running brook, on a big leaf, open your pill-box of jam, carve your paddle—in fact to set your table.

What's the use of all this trouble unless you put on a little style?

Cod Fish Cakes

½ cup or "fistful" of flaked codfish.

50-50 with the fish—mashed potatoes.

Mix. Pinch of salt—maybe. (Cod is often very salty. This may be soaked out of it at home.)

Thimble-full of melted butter.

A very small jolt of "egg powder" or part of a real egg (¼). Carry this mixture in your Baby Bag, wrapped in oiled paper. Arrived at the feeding ground: Rig your pail for "deep fat." Danger! Stir in a little milk now, and do not make your cakes too soft. Roll them in flour —and lower into very hot fat to cover. Look out! Hot fat burns like hot iron. Clumsy Jack-knifers pass this up, please. It is a luxurious dish with baked beans.

Yankee diet!

If you own the Boy Scout's Cook Kit fry-pan, pail, dish, cup and knife and fork—this combination is easy. Beans in pail overnight underground. Serve with fish-cakes in the morning!

Pitfalls: Cakes crumble, stick in the pan, are soggy with fat, of a sickly color, too salty. Not enough milk, not enough potato; fat not deep enough or hot enough. For a gang this recipe is: 2 cups Cod, flaked or fluffed Cod. 2 cups mashed potato. ½ teaspoon salt (?) 2 tablespoons melted butter. 1 egg. *Milk.*

Chili-con-carne

Soaked and boiled red beans with chopped beef, tomatoes, peppers and onions. Fry onions first, in the bottom of the pail. Then tripod the pail and when beans and tomatoes and peppers have simmered for a whole morning—drop in the beef—and cook for hours more. Salt to taste. Adding a bay-leaf, rosemary, chopped ginger-root (just enough—only pinches) makes this cowboy dish stand right up on its hind legs and yell to be eaten. (See Condiments.)

Slow Cooking—Pot Roast, "en casserole" and other fancy dishes. Chicken, meat game,—with vegetables and *seasonings*—cooked with the pot, covered in a little water. Add chopped celery, dried mushrooms from the grocer (*Note!* Some mushrooms are deadly poison, but Puff Balls, Beeksteak and Coral Mushrooms are safe—study them up in the Town Library—and add a leaf to your book of knowledge) and some flour thickening (sometimes)—in your pail on a tripod for a couple of hours, or more, tasting and testing it for tenderness and flavor! Very slowly!

Poulet en casserole sounds great! Chicken with vegetables cooked slowly.

Chop Suey — Everything edible — cooked slowly.

Valenciana—We called it General Cargo in Spanish Guam, 1897.

Pork scraps reduced with onions in a huge earthen pot (our pot will do), chicken cooked to tender in this, with a little water, and the top on. Then you add rice until you cover the chicken—

"VALENCIANA"

dry unwashed rice. Let it steam. Then add green peas, dried mushrooms, peeled almonds, artichoke hearts, olives, a little tomato, a sweet red pepper . . . and let it steam some more, adding water when you see it needs more, and cook and cook and *cook*. When Devisse came in with this, on Thursday Noons, all conversation ceased.

Put good things into the pail, cook slow, and you can't go wrong, as I said before.

RICE

We Foreign Devils hang on to the flour bag when in a tight place—but our Chinese and Japanese pals hang on to *rice*. How wonderfully and easily they cook it! Not a sticky mess, oozing water—but fluffy, snowy—all the grains separate!

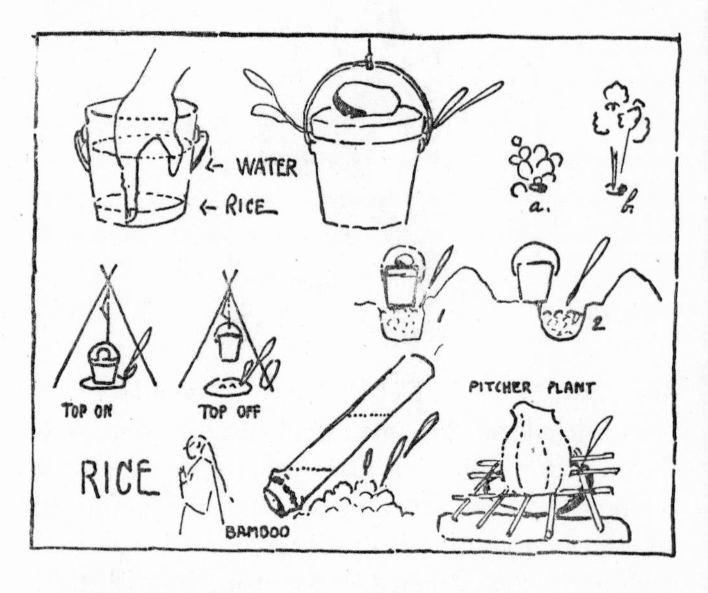

Chinese and Japanese rice is different—but it is cooked the same way. You have a very "brisk" bed of coals ready. You take a fistful of rice and wash it until the milky water has gone clear, if in running water. Six washings for poured water. Drain off the water. Put your rice in the big pail and add four times the amount of salted water. To be sure Japs always guess at this and Ah Siew, the Chinese Cook we had at home said "Lice one; water dree nikles." He meant the rice must reach the first joint (knuckle) of your finger—the water must reach to the third knuckle. Cover the pail and bring it to boil. The cover will dance, so put a clean stone atop to hold it down. In about 15 or 20 minutes it will *suddenly stop* dancing. At this sign *take off the lid.* You will soon make out a score or so of tiny volcanoes all spouting bubbles. When the bubbles turn to jets of steam "draw your fire"; that is, "hoist away handsomely on your lard-pail halyards." In landlubber lingo: gently get your pot higher up. Never stir or jar the rice while cooking it! Your rice must now be kept steaming, drying on a *very* gentle fire, where it may stay until wanted. If it stays one minute on a hot fire after those bubbles go you *have burned it.*

In Borneo I noted rice cooked in bamboo joints. In a pitcher-plant—and one boy in Ogden, in a prize contest, *said* he cooked rice on a flat stone, down in a Baby Imu or Plug-hat Hole. He wet the rice and carefully lowered it down into the Imu. Covered it. In one hour he had a rice cake—well cooked. This was topnotch Jack-Knifing!

Plum Duff

To your twister and chupatty-dough add milk, seeded raisins, currants, pitted prunes, chopped up fine. Fistful of sugar, ditto suet (butter will make it soggy) some pinches of nutmeg, mace (salt and B. P. already)—maybe chopped candied fruit? Stew or tie it up in double cheese-cloth, and slip it into your pot when merrily boiling. Let her bile at least *all afternoon* not too fast else you'll be feeding it more water instead of catching fish or having other fun. For a hard sauce mix butter and sugar with a pinch of cinnamon. For a syrupy sauce *melt* sugar and butter plus cinnamon. Oh, Boy!

Short Cake

Make two chupatties with milk (not water) and sugar, baking powder little more than usual, and less salt, but some. When done, toast them all. Now butter them, all sides. Into your pot goes a layer of blueberries *or* wild strawberries, or cherries, with sugar scattered over. Then a split chupatty. Then more berries and sugar. Then another chupatty—till your pot is full. Put on cover, sink in the Plug-hat Hole, cover with branches, leaves, earth. Go about your other fun. *In an hour—Be Patient* for once—turn all out on a plate (we'll have to have one for Short Cake) and—you know.

This can be made with apples, peaches, pears —raw or dried. Alas, if dry fruit is used you must soak and cook first—'t ain't so good!

Use plenty of blueberries! Lots of sugar! It won't poison you—not if you keep hopping around.

Rice Pudding

One egg beaten up. ½ cup of milk. Cup of cooked rice. Currants or raisins (if nobody cares, *plenty*). Place in your smallest pail or cup and arrange it over your big pail so as to steam it. This is a Bain Marie, or double-boiler. This goes quickly; in 15 minutes it ought to be ready. Good cold.

Custard

One egg, sugar, a little milk. Cook in a Bain Marie (double boiler), dust in a pinch or two of flour and stir until it gets "oily" or like molasses. Then cool in the brook.

Sauces

Stir a tablespoon of flour in your iron fry-pan over the coals, until a golden brown. Then add 50-50 butter. Let cook a moment. Now pour in boiling water, little by little (stirring hard) until it all swells up like (for it *is*) gravy. It won't lump if your water is boiling. Season with salt, chopped parsley, pepper.

Brown Sauce or Gravy

Use the drippings from skillet steak, or fresh blood or beef fat. If you use bacon fat or salt pork fat, don't salt it. Sift flour, not too much, into it, stir. Flour must cook for about 1 minute. Then add some boiling water and *stir*. Cook three minutes. Brown with burnt sugar. Season "high."

Flapjacks

Made with our old Twister recipe, unless we buy a package of ready-to-mix kind, but here you must have a fry-pan. You must discover the exact heat to fry cakes in the field. A dying bed of coals is the best. You drop your flapjacks on a good and hot, lightly greased pan and flip them when you see the bubbles beginning to "set." (To toss or flip a Flapjack practise up with the lid of your pail or a big chip in the fry-pan before you get it hot.) Fire does it. Pound the ashes down if too hot or sift more ashes over them. The only way is to experiment. The Plug Hat works well when you have mastered it. If your coals are tuned down to the right heat you may rest the fry-pan square on the coals. Make a swab to grease the pan.

The first cake should be as good as the last. Is it ever so?

French Toast

Very popular and easy to hand out to a hungry crowd in a hurry. Beat up some eggs, soak sliced bread in this and fry like pancakes. Salt, cream, milk, and some sugar make this better. Maple syrup!

Corn Cakes

Fresh corn, boiled ten minutes . . . or until tender . . . and cut off the cob, ½ cup; white flour, ½ cup; butter, ½ teaspoon. Baking Powder one level teaspoon and salt, ¼ teaspoon. You must get smart at measuring by fistsful, pinches and so on. Add milk or water slowly.

Buckwheat and *Flannel Cakes* come in a package. Heavy to tote but light to eat.

Rice Cakes

Fifty-fifty cooked rice and flour, plus your baking powder, salt and sugar. Just enough to make a cupful or two fistsful. A few currants tucked into the batter seem to "go good." Ration for two strong boys.

Crêpe

Pronounced to rhyme with Scrape. Very thin, waxy pan-cakes eaten heated up with a fancy syrup. To one cup of flour add salt, ¼ spoon, butter, 1 spoon, and thin to a batter with milk. Milk powder and water will do. Then add TWO EGGS, beaten well with a swizzle stick or a fork, if you have one.

A swizzle stick is merely a three-pronged twig, whirled between your palms.

Fry in a generous swabbing of butter, on not too hot a pan. They are poured thin and when done placed in a pile. Now put a little lemon and orange juice, and sugar in the pan with butter, some water, and as it comes to a boil swab the pan with the zest or outside peel of the lemons and oranges you have used. Tip the pan a little for this stunt. When the sugar is melted and the syrup is just right, not too watery that is, dip a crêpe into it, let it sizzle a moment, then roll it up and destroy by eating. Sounds very difficult but my ten-year-old caddy, down in Tunisia, could make one per minute. When he bade me good-bye he blubbered "Adieu, Monsieur de Crêpe" showing that he had always called me that behind my back. I didn't mind!

Crêpes are grand at a picnic. For the honor of your family name go ahead and spoil a few hundred pounds of flour, crates of eggs, and an acre or two of second-growth hickory. One successful batch of crêpes will elect you a life member of the Jack-knifers and win you many friends.

Pfan Kucke

Make a batter as for twisters. Then make your fry-pan hot, butter it well, including the sides. Pour in a lot of batter, enough to cover bottom and sides of your pan. This is best made on a "flamey" fire of small dry stuff. Turn the pan so that the batter runs up the sides of the pan. When done, pry it out. This cake has a fence

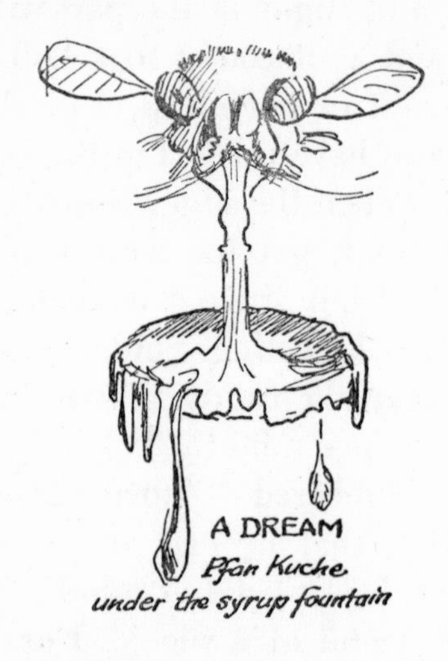

around it to hold a syrup made of sugar and a pinch of cinnamon. Swamp it in syrup—Here's your chance! Then get outside of it!

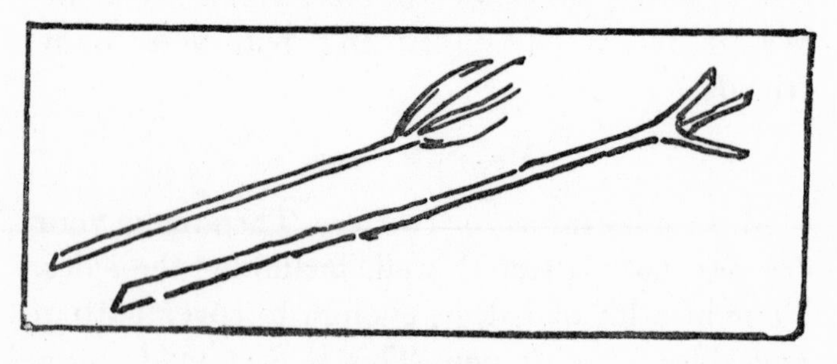

A Swizzle Stick

THE CONDIMENT CAN

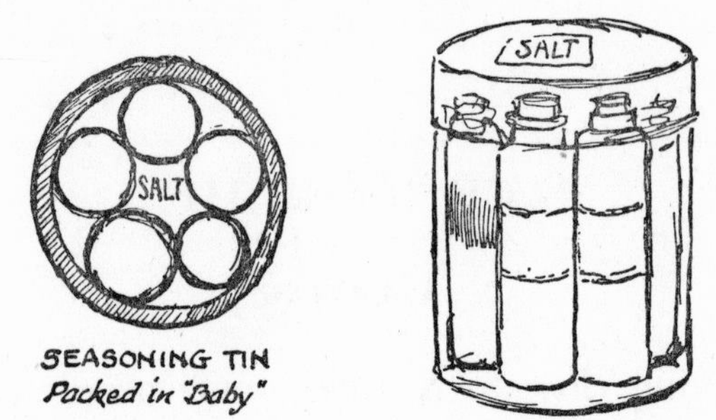

"BABY" IS CANADIAN FOR "RATION BAG"

Seasoning. Salt, pepper, spices . . . these should be added very carefully to food. You ought to just barely taste your seasoning. Give the food a chance.

So! Now learn all the above and you'll be able to say "I'm getting on."

Kabobs! Twisters! 'n' everything!

Poor boy! You are only a *third* baked. For besides Cooking there are also Camping and First Aid. All three necessary for your proper bringing up.

CHAPTER III

Camping

Living close to Nature—some people call it! Not too close! You must know how to be as comfortable and happy as the old girl, Mother Nature, will allow, under the circumstances. Sleeping, or trying to, on cold ground or damp is getting too near—or letting in mosquitoes (showing that Mrs. Mosquito has more brains than you have) or the rain (Jupiter Pluvius) or putting up with any *avoidable* discomfort.

Still keeping our unit of *one* on the Desert Island let us see how one boy can *camp* and get the best fun out of it. You may double-up with a pal or two, maybe more, at any time, and divide the work and share the joys. One for one then changes to "One for all—All for one." (See chapter on the Gang.) After years and years of worry, accidents, scrapes, and, may I add, *expenses,* I, at last, settled on a sort of method—an outfit and a program for pick-a-back camping. To go and live high where even ponies cannot scramble—to say nothing of motor-cars! Up to ten years ago this "fit-out" was subject to change; (this régime, my style of camping) like the program in a circus. There are so many ways of beating or rather coaxing Mother Nature to behave, that I tried everybody's way and now "my way" is a grand mixture of everybody's. The books I read! At the feet of how many scarred veterans have I not sat? "Tell me, Master," I would ask, "what did you do *then?*" Never an old sport but would tell me his experience. Then I tried it on the only dog I dared to face—myself. Valleys, mountains, meadows—dry as dust, wet, sweltering and shivering—bogged, flooded, baked. All but snow and ice. I am leaving that for my old age.

TRANSPORT, BOARD AND LODGING!

When you are your own pack-horse, your own cook and waiter, your own house-builder. Until you strike out for yourself on a week-end camp tramp, you don't know the meaning of *adventure.*

Transport means moving to get somewhere with the baggage. *Lodging* means a dry, snug house and a *fairly* soft bed. *Board* means good, proper food, properly cooked. Are these enough? No sir! The Jack-knifer must have a code.

A code is a way of thinking and doing and

is written inside of your skull, where nobody can see it. Boys' skulls are small—so I advise you to have your code short and comprehensive. Boil it down to two words and you can't go far wrong. Be kind: to *yourself* first, for your body is the temple of your race. Don't play the jackass with your wonderful body! Be kind to your pals —mother and father and other pals. That means to serve. Be kind to good old Mother Nature— That means Preserve and Conserve. Fight to keep all that is beauty in yourself, your friends and in Nature. Two words are *plenty*.

As I write, a caravan of desert Bedouins have come to a halt near my "villa." Sixteen camels loaded with tentage, poles, sacks, pots, pans, women, babies and dogs. It's a tribe just in from the Sahara Desert. They rest for a while. Then all hands turn-to and presto! A village appears. I notice nobody interferes with anybody else— all have inherited a certain job in the building of this little city. The camels grunt, bawl, wail! The dogs, mean ones, smelling me, an "unbeliever," as I lean over the wall, are barking furiously. But calmly and quietly with scarcely an order given, up go the camel's-hair blanket-tents, a wall of brush is dragged into place, the fires are lighted and the fumes of cous-cous waft down the breeze. Appears Mahomet, my cook. "These Bedouins will steal everything off your place.

Monsieur. We must have a day and night watchman." There! You see? No *code.*

But what a wonderful piece of *camping!* Centuries—thousands of years old—*method.*

INTRODUCING WILLIAM J. APPLEDIP, SCIENTIFIC PICKABACK CAMPER

The following two-act Pantomime-playlet was written some years ago and is performed annually in a stadium near Honolulu. Into it is compressed a whole lot about *codes, outfit, transportation, cookery* and *hygiene* for one small boy on a week-end hike. And some "fun." With copious footnotes to make it *very scientific.*

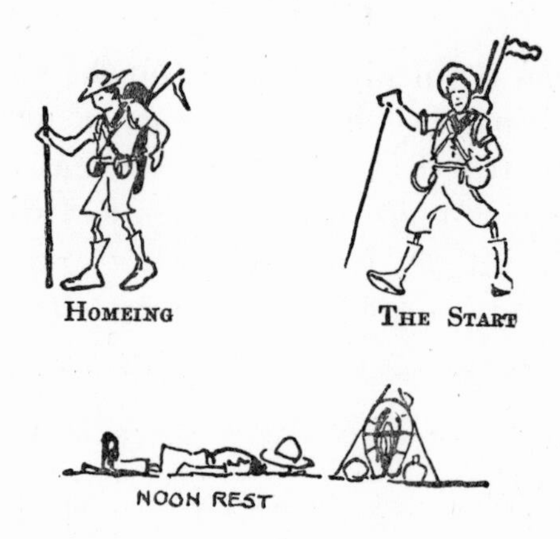

CHAPTER IV

Billy Appledip

Act I—Scene I

Dramatis Personae

William J. Appledip.........By Himself
Bimbo ....By Bimbo

WILLIAM APPLEDIP AND HIS OUTFIT

William Appledip[a] appears on the scene. He wears a broad-brimmed hat,[b] blue woolen shirt[c] with gay red neckerchief.[d] On a leather belt[e] swings a jack-knife.[f] Also, a hank[g] of straw-size cord, one fathom long. He wears grey woolen soccer[i] pants[j] sawed off just above the knee.

a. His picture is from life. Watch him. He may be President some day! No joke!

b. Your hat should be stiff enough to fan your coals, shed rain. Mark in indelible ink inside, on the felt, with your name and address. No borrower can stand seeing that name forty times a day.

c. All wool. Wash it only in water almost too hot to hold your hand in, with soap shavings, by dousing it up and down in the suds. Rinse (don't wring it) in clean luke-warm water. Hang

In the Arena

up to dry without wringing. When perfectly dry, iron with clean fry-pan filled with coals. For an ironing board fold your tent on a flat place and spread your towel over it. Don't economize on your shirt. Get the *best.* Two handkerchief pockets, one for compass, one for First Aid kit.

d. Should be two cubits square. (See Jack-knife scale.) This keeps your upper spine cool in hot weather, warm in cold. Some of its uses are:

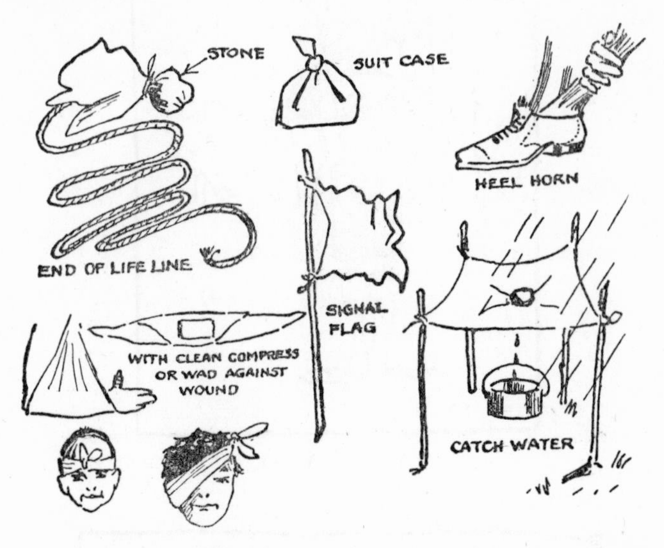

1. An arm, head knee support bandage. 2. Dress-suit case. 3. Table napkins. 4. Mosquito and Fly bar. 5. As a warning signal for deer hunters who have a way of banging at any moving thing in the woods. It should be used often, washed often and rinsed, as above. After ironing hang it in the sun. See First Aid.

e. Belt. Leather or woven, with two inserted rings for knife and lanyard.

f. Jack-knife. Frankly, the Boy Scout Knife is just right in my opinion. (See p. 15.)

Blade, Reamer, Screwdriver, Soda-bottle opener and can-opener. A good knife has for close partner a small whetstone—one inch by two. Kept in a home-made leather case, and tucked in a pocket. Soak it for days in oil to finish it. Hold the blade at about 20° angle for a good cutting edge. Then strop it on the inside of your belt. In using a real knife, razor sharp, think of your arteries, your tendons and discount chances for those permanent scars some men carry on hands and fingers; signs of the American born.

g. The Hank. Indispensable! Buy the small size cord used to hoist the veranda shades. Big as an average straw—not macaroni size. When you have to wait somewhere unsling your hank and tie knots. Begin with "the Knot Universal" the half hitch. Next, the running half-hitch.

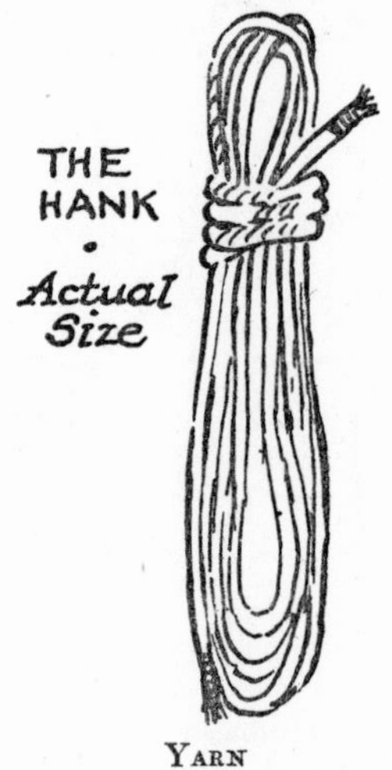

YARN

A native cowboy (name withheld—he's dead now, anyway) came into camp late, once, at Ulupalakua, a glorious old ranch on the sportsman's island, Maui (Hawaii, U. S. A.—integral U. S. like Martha's Vineyard or Catalina. *Not* a possession!) He was all scratched up and so was his mustang—a descendant of horses brought to us in 1795—long before "Cowboys" were heard of on the mainland. This was his story.

"Me and my horse comes to a pali (cliff) and this horse I had on, he don't jump. He's bin afraid and me too to break a leg.

I cinch him up good! I tie lass (lasso!) on pommel, and one end around a sree (tree) I blind him (blindfold) and shove him off! Lower away! Then I slide down too, on de lass. Here we bin." (Here we are.)

"Is this the lass?"

"Sure."

(We small boys all from Missouri.)

"Did you go back?"

"No."

(Aha! Now we had him.)

"Then how did you get back your lass?"

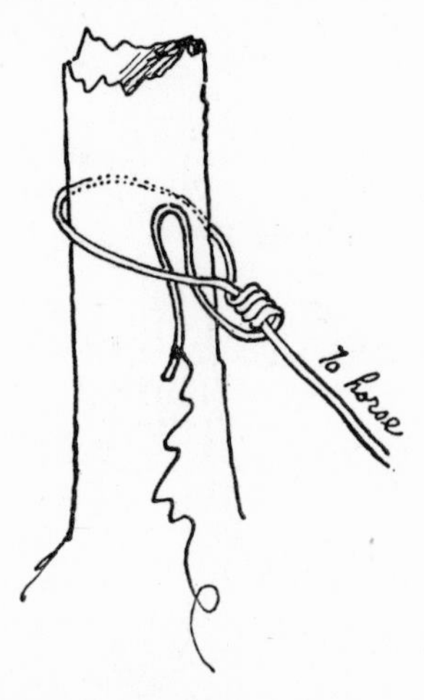

He never flinched but produced the lasso and a *hank of cod-line* (used for catching Ulua, a much regarded big fish that grubs along the shore) and tied a funny knot, which I'll call "the running-half-hitch-hangman's-bowline-on-a-bight." With this cod-line tied to A, after his horse had been lowered, kicking down the cliff, the cowboy (so he said) came down the rope (B) and then yanked in the fish line (A) until the loop (bight) at C worked out. He then pulled on his "lass" until it worked loose and gave way. I hereby give this knot to posterity—for I have never seen or heard of it since. It was invented for an emergency —which is the very acme of Jack-knifery.

Blue golf stockings[k] and laced walking shoes.[l] On his back he carries a 25 lb. pack:[m] Tent,[n]

But to resume. Get a book on knots.

g. See p. 163 Jack-knife scale.

i. Soccer pants. Of whipcord or wool.

j. Have always been worn by mountain climbers, "Tyroleans," Soccer, and Basket Ballers and should be adopted by athletes in general (except Base Ball and Football players) as giving the knee a square deal—that is, *room to work.* They are cheap, too, and one pair of good stuff outlasts three pairs of long "pants."

Two hip-pockets. Handkerchief in right one, note-book and pencil in left. Query, why? (Work it out—you'll see.) Two side pockets. Left contains small Kit bag: flat, with threaded needle, flat bobbin of stout thread. Piece of string. Bit of wax. Matches in Gillette Razor case, etc. Right hand pocket for *rubbish:* such as one dead crab, two horrible "all day suckers" and purse, containing, if you're lucky, a quarter in nickels. Two deep watch pockets—left, whetstone. Right, a *watch.* What underwear? Light wool "athletics," even in summer. "Damp cotton underwear keeps the boys' graveyard full," says Mrs. McGillicuddy and she brought up sixteen. (In winter wear long trousers with your *light woolen* underwear, heavy over-coat and muffler.)

k. Wool.

l. Laced walking shoes. Thick and big enough not to squeeze your feet in thick stockings. The lacing is valuable for making fire in a scrape, without matches, so have them of leather. Paint them once a year with lamb's tallow, 1 oz.; resin, a pinch; beeswax ½ oz. Then the tops will last forever.

m. Two straps over shoulders padded with something soft where they grind against your bones. (See Pack diagrams.) 25 pounds would be very light—the weight all depends upon how husky you are.

n. Tent. I recommend the tent issued by the Boy Scouts of America, catalogued as a very light "Canoe" tent. Weight 3½ lbs. size 6 x 4 x 4. Made of very tough, waterproof stuff, with mosquito bar attachment. Carry your poles along . . . it pays in the long run. Dowel rods. Saves the saplings!

The canoe tent has a round end which at first bothers the

novice. Set it up near home and tie strings of the exact length between A and B in the picture to give you this distance for a while, until you get used to pitching it smoothly. The Pup Ranger

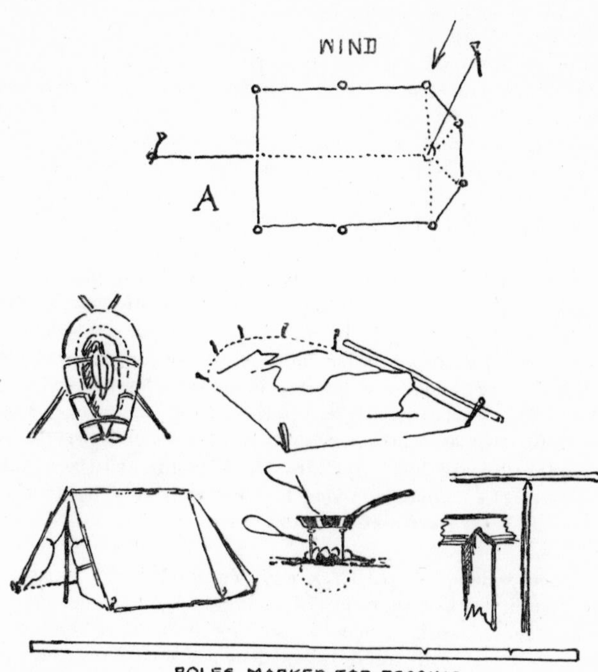

SOME OF APPLEDIP'S OUTFIT

or Jack-knifer Tent is easy to handle, for you may peg them *as you unroll them.* So fold them correctly and save time (see p. 93).

Four-inch nails, or longer, may be permanently attached to the bottom. That pays too.

Folding the Canoe Tent. Be sure your nail pegs are all pointing one way, as you fold and roll this tent, or you are likely to tear holes in it.

You can use an old U. S. Army Pup-tent if there are no mosquitoes or flies on your desert island. Here above are rough plans for a simple, home-made *Pup:*

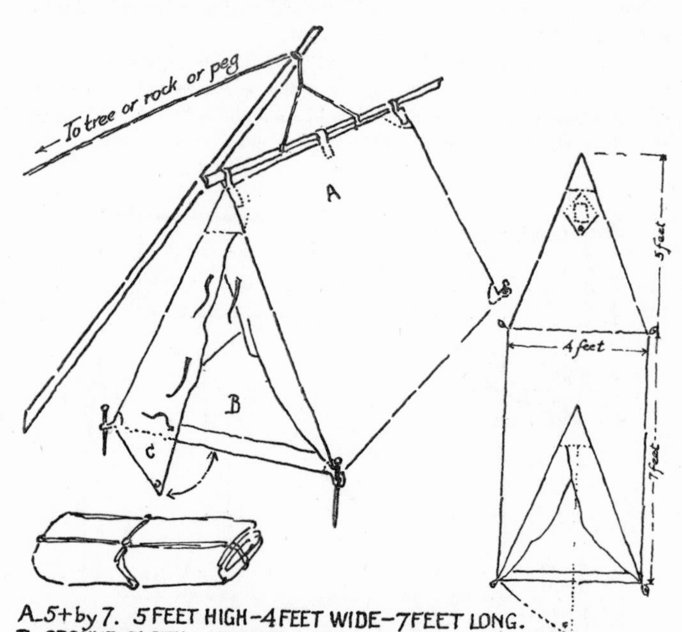

A_5+ by 7. 5 FEET HIGH–4 FEET WIDE–7 FEET LONG.
B_GROUND CLOTH. 4 FEET BY 7 FEET. CANVAS.
C_WHEN OPEN ON WINDWARD SIDE. WHEN TENT IS CLOSED "C" TUCKS UNDER GROUND CLOTH, (USE A STICK) AND, TAPES TIED, MAKES "PUP RANGE" RAT, DOG AND PORCUPINE PROOF.

THE PUP RANGER OR "JACK-KNIFER"

Use Egyptian Cotton, fine and light, water-proofed with paraffin wax, rubbed on and ironed in. Make it a foot longer than you are . . . and allow for growing. Seven feet long is roomy.

If you ever want to camp in grand comfort use a two-man "Range" tent when weight does not count. This is described on page 95 with drawings.

The Range Tent. This is not in any catalogue that I have but any Awning and Tentmaker will make it for you. Eight feet high, pyramid, with stout sewed-in ground canvas, 7 by 7, with a bug or snake fence across the door. This sheds torrential rain and flaps of the door tie up. Dog proof.

Has a rear window for ventilation, made mosquito proof by pinning netting over it. Goes up in many ways, as you see. Made of Egyptian it would be almost light enough to "tote" meanwhile it is just the thing for an auto or pack mule trip. 10 lbs.

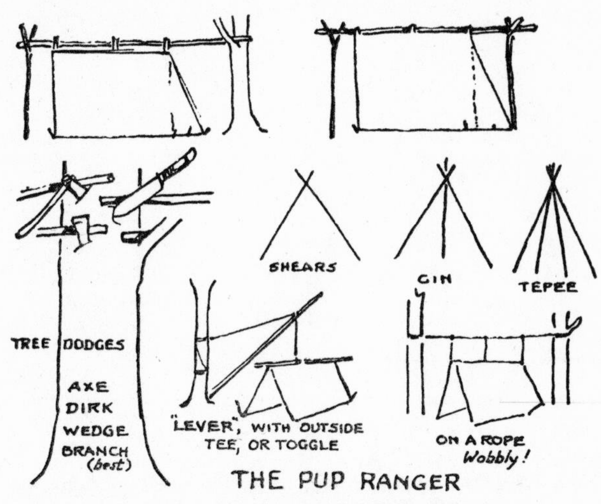

WITH SOME OUTDOOR "DODGES"

This is the most comfortable one or two man tent I ever used. On pegging down over browse or hay your bed is under the floor . . . minus the beetles, ants and other crawling bed-fellows. Goes up in all sorts of ways, quick as a wink. Outside shears, outside gin or tripod, inside or outside four-pod and inside single pole. For the latter you must guy against the wind. In a storm rig the inside four-pod, cut to fit the inside angles of the pyramid. This stops all flapping, usually that boresome snapping of fire crackers that you hear when camping on the reef in the Trade Wind belt.

My own rig is the *Lever* which you will find in the accompanying diagrams. This allows more elbow room inside the tent but has its disadvantages . . . which you will find out for yourself. The sewed-in ground cloth gets damp in time, but by easing out

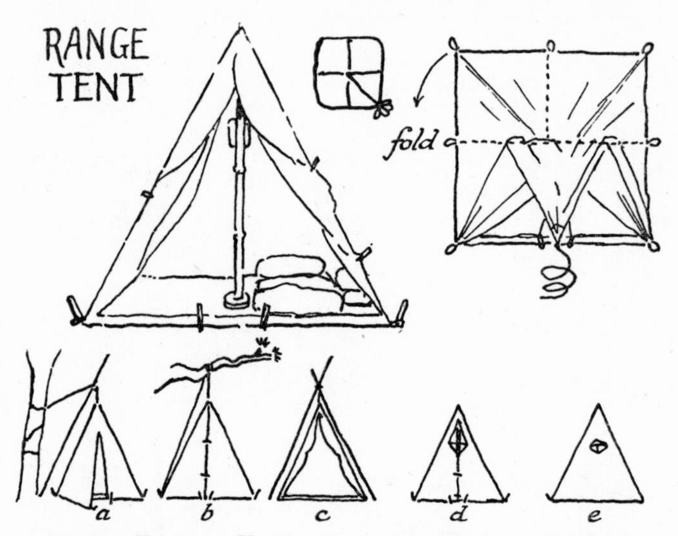

A. HANDY TREE; B. HANDY "LIVE" BRANCH; C. "SHEARS"; D. INSIDE POLE; E. REAR VIEW, WITH VENTILATOR WINDOW.

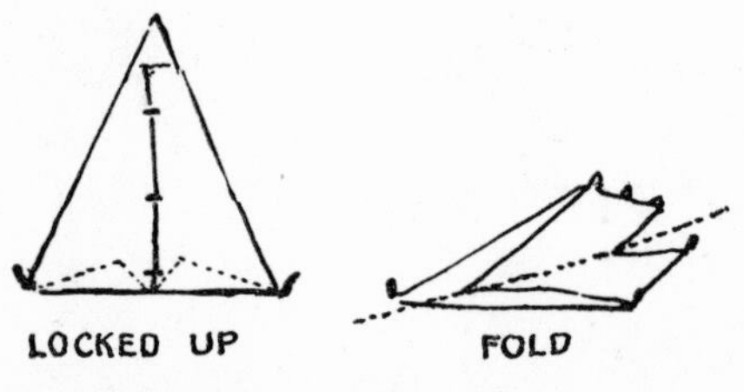

the front pegs and pulling the tent back, a morning's sunshine will fix that. Then, in both the Range and the Pup Range (or shall we call it the Jack-knifer?) one does not lose all the clothes pins and safety pins the very first night by leaving them in the grass.

Folding up the Range Tent. Begin by letting down your poles, or striking poles, as the saying is. Then, with tent-pegs still in

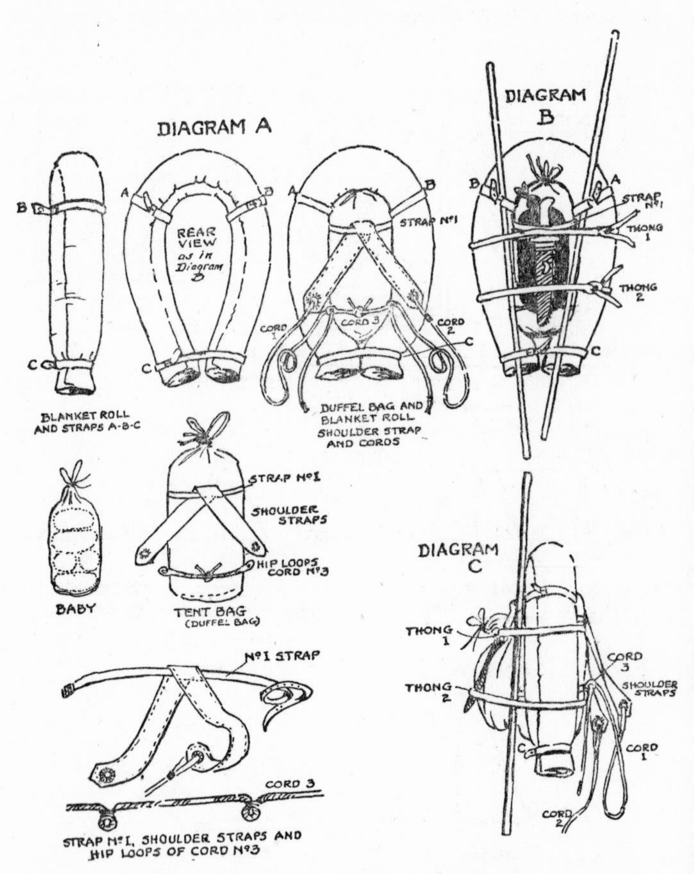

THE PACK, POLES, BABY AND STRAPS

the ground, fold as in the cut, page 95, getting your edges tucked in all square. Take up front tent-pegs, stow them in your rope-bag, to save your tent from getting dirty, and then pull up your dirk,[o] two short poles,[p] middle finger size; a blanket[q] and ground cloth[r] (Poncho) roll[s] and ration bag or "The Baby."[t] A quart canteen[u] hangs on his left,[v] a mess kit (pail, plate, fry-pan, cup, spoon and fork in a case)[w] hangs over right shoulder.[x] Under his arm he holds a bull[y] pup. His picture is on page 87.

back pegs. Fold over with an eye to having only the under side of the ground-cloth exposed. Your tent will stay white for a long time.

The Ranger Tent must have poles—long ones, for the outside, but only one for the *inside* as on page 95. Sometimes you do not *need any*.

To return to Bill Appledip's outfit. O. See Dirk, pages 55 and 56. P. See Poles diagram page 96. Q. Blanket, is rolled up in the poncho with pyjamas, extra clothes and moccasins inside. Strapped

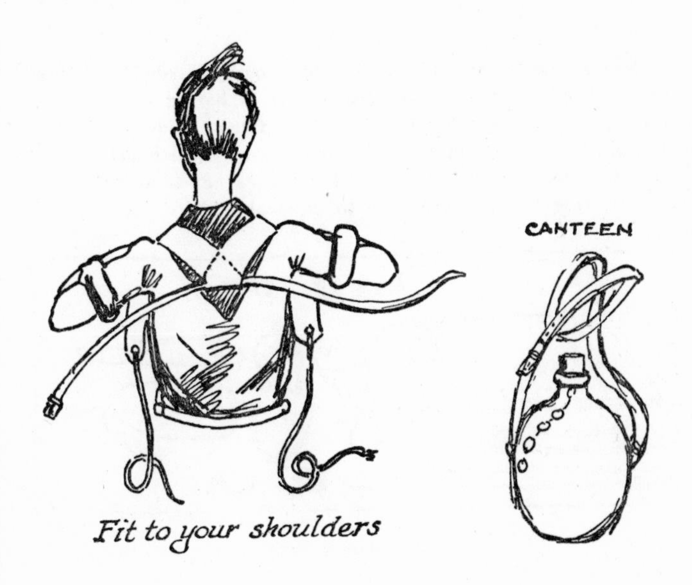

up horseshoe shape the tent is jammed into the middle, the whole snugged with two long, soft leather thongs: chrome tanned are best. Then the shoulder straps! These are not on the market so you must make them yourself. Buy a strip of sail-cloth 18 inches long and 3 inches wide. Fold over into a hollow and sew. Turn inside out. Fold it over a strap (Strap 1) and fit it to your shoulders. See diagrams. This is very important, so pay attention.

Some boys take a right angle, some an acute angle. (Diagram A, p. 96.) You'll thank me some day after a long hike for all of this. These shoulder straps make a pack feel light, especially if lined with soft material like flannel. Strap one is a woven strap with buckle—on which your pack hangs as it goes around and cinches your tent-bag near the top. Two "straw-size" sash cords, 18 inches long or longer and whipped carefully (B) go under your arms from the grommets or "eyelets" in your shoulder straps (C) ... to strap No. 2—(which has two rings sewn or loops tied in it)—fastened with a running half-hitch or even more loosely. You see, you might want to drop your pack in a hurry. One slight yank on a string should be enough. This is scientific!

Yarn

Charley Norton and I were climbing over Waiahole in 1908. Very steep. We both foresaw the danger of having a pack stick when suddenly wanted off. His was a fancy "Limousine" bag with a sort of mule harness, with all sorts of buckles and straps, bought in New York. It was raining great guns and Charley slipped. One doesn't have time to unbuckle things when falling

Makings of a Pack

head-over heels down a precipice. I know it now, but it took that adventure with Charley Norton to rub it in. When I got nerve enough to move I looked down (30 feet!) among the tree-ferns and Palapalai, and saw him all of a huddle. After a while he stirred. So I called weakly "Are you there?" "Yes, I am," said he, "But I feel like a wish bone that has been wished with." The pack had twisted him, but not fatally.

Moral: Digest this.

Your blanket being rolled in your ground cloth (as in Diagram, Page 96), you jam your tent bag into it. It must fit tight. Now tie all up snug with your long thongs, 1 and 2. (B) Pull the pucker-string of your Baby (food bag) through a strap (No. 1) and let it hang over so rain can't enter. Screw in your tent-poles, under all the straps and thongs and your dirk (or axe, if you can't get a dirk)—under, and there you are! The flag you see in the cut was Billy Appledip's own addition and it went over big. He also suggested looping cords 1 and 2 under the lower ends of the tent poles. "Well, that's a good way, too."

Blanket. Why do they cost so like sixty? But get a good one and have it gay—Red and White stripes look cheerful. Some men say "Have it square and lie cat-a-cornered." This gives you a fold-over for your feet and some extra blanket for your pillow. The size of your blanket determines that of your pack.

Pillow. Your pillow is your tent-bag stuffed with clothes or hay. Keep out the crickets—they sound like elephants crawling inside next your ear. *R.* Ground-cloth. Three yards of gay-colored oil-cloth. Doesn't last long, but it is cheap. Bigger than the blanket. *S.* The roll. When your blanket and ground-cloth have aired—roll them as in diagram A, p. 96, tight. The overlap is to the rear, well over, to shed water. Straps must fit. Better *get ready*—it pays. Unless this pack fits you and is "assembled" right *for you* it is worse than carrying a basket of eggs—uncomfortable and rickety. *T.* Ration Bag. Draw-string on a small bag, about 9 by 18 inches, of water-proofed cotton. Smear with melted paraffin and then iron it in. This is what to carry in it. A seasoning tin, in which you carry some salt and pepper, a small bottle of "soy," or Worcestershire or A1 Sauce. Pinches of Rosemary, Thyme, Cinnamon and Nutmeg in Homeopathic Medicine bottles packed in the salt. All these give dishes "distinction" when used with art. They make *drab* cooking taste like Ciro's at Monte

Carlo. Some folks don't like them. Our Grandmothers did, however, and that may explain the horrible home cooking in the Average American Home. Your "baby" see diagram 17, p. 96, must hold a small tin of grease—vegetable lard—a small bag of flour, a small tin of butter, a tin of jam and whatever you think you'll want for lunch, or dinner or breakfast—or all three. Your baking powder is already sifted into your flour if you like. Your "baby" will hold meals for a week-end hike. After that you must buy as you go. *U.* Canteen. Aluminum, which allows you to boil suspicious water in your canteen itself, for thirty minutes at least. Stagnant water

has been made sweet by boiling it with condensed milk and then strained. Read the chapter on *Water.* The canteen is used as a hot-water bag, for your feet, on a cold night. As a coffee pot, for cocoa, tea. Scald it often. If it is cased in felt you may cool your water, on a hot day, by hanging it up wet, in a breezy place. *W.* Mess Kit. If you can stand the price buy the *aluminium* outfit recommended by the Boy Scouts of America and sold by their Supply Department, 200 Fifth Avenue, New York. But a second-hand U. S. Army mess-kit, in a bag, with strap is good; knife, fork and spoon inside. Carry a pint cup, for your stew, tied on your pack. A lard pail *will* do if you are very poor. *Y.* Under his arm, a Bull Pup. Billy Appledip's was made of

He limps, for he is footsore after seven miles[z] hike. He hobbles up to the grand stand and salutes[A1] the Governor of the state. This first-class statesman returns the salute, and watches[A2] every move of this rising star from now on.[A3]

William—call him Bill—chooses his camp site[A4] with care. Notes,[A5] by wet finger,[A6] direction of the wind.[A7] Looks aloft like a wise sea-captain to note the kind of weather as told by the clouds.[A8] Finds a grass-covered gravel[A9] site with good drainage.[A10] unships (1) Dog[B1] (2) Pack[B2] (3) Mess Kit[B3] (4) Canteen[B4] Pours water into hand[B5] and gives dog a drink.[B6] Notices dog is lame. Brings out First Aid Kit. Bandages up dog's leg. Takes a pull[D1] at canteen and spits out[D2] water. Breaks out Cook Kit and Ration Bag or "Baby."[D3] Drives three six-inch wire nails[D4] in a place four yards from his camp-site, down wind.[D5]

lath, paper and some wire. He *saluted* when you pulled his tail! But you are entitled to a real one. A dog, like a horse, boat, or camel, is educational. Your dog reflects your own character, just as you reflect your Dad's or your Scoutmaster's. *Z.* Seven miles! You can *work up to it,* but it is a long, long walk. It tests your shoes, socks, feet. Be sure you are "scientific" here, and never start off with new shoes! Pare your nails ship-shape, hands and feet. A1. The Governor saluted—of course. He knows the Jack-knife breed, Scout breed, Demolay breed—and, I dare say, ignores the knifeless, non-whittling, uncreative sort of fellow. But to resume:

NOTE: A2 Salutes. Raises his hat. If he belongs to a society chartered by Congress, as are Scouts and Seascouts, for example, he will salute with his hand, hat on. Local in one case. National in the other. A3. One good Appledip can sell the idea of "Self-Reliant though Human" to everyone who sees him at work at home or abroad. A poor specimen, on the other hand, hampers us all. "Bedouin," *unsells* the idea. That's all!

A4. Bad camp sites make harder work—sometimes we must camp where we can. There's the camp site in a wilderness of smoking bricks, for instance, or on the mud-flats after a flood. The boy who can camp *there*—ah! That reminds me!

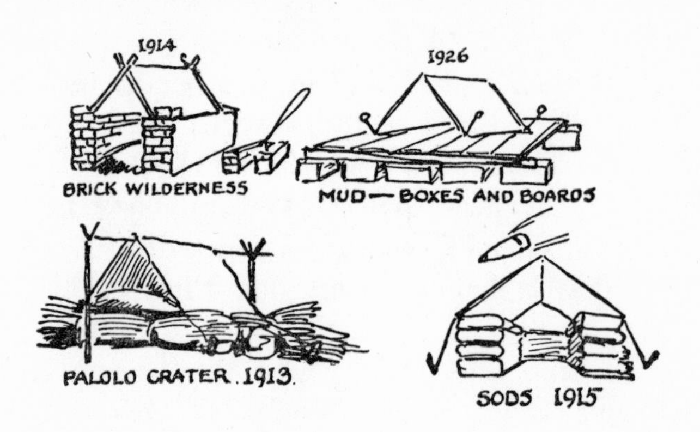

YARN

We came to the crater about sundown. It was like a huge bowl with an unexpected lake in the middle, four inches deep in water, already, and still raining pitchforks. The Sachem thought: Too late to go back. Too wet to camp. No dry ground or wood. Sixteen youngsters—all Mother's darlings. What can I do?" Called a council. "Go back?" Chorus: "No!" (think quick, Sachem, think quick!) "Then *stay*"*!* (Cheers.) There was a heavy patch of rushes growing in the centre, where there had always been a little water. "Out Jack-knives, all hands, and cut rushes while the light lasts." So spake in thunder tones the great (but shaky) Sachem. Where the water was barely an inch deep we piled the rushes on a layer of guava branches. On this "raft" we pitched our pup tents. For fire we cut into the underside of a dead, slanting and hollow Koa-tree (kind of mahogany) and making fine chips, *tooth-picks,* of the dry part, soon had a glorious fire, which dried and burned into wet wood. On this, one boy, sheltered by a poncho, grilled our jerked beef. That and a preboiled potato was our supper. Preboiled—boiled at home before we started, of course. We undressed outside, in the pelting rain. Inside our tents we gingerly broke out our ponchos, blankets, warm woolen pyjamas. Our tents were bunched, two boys in one, so we sang and told stories while the tropic rain hurled down on us in vain. Next day was sunny and we erected a "wicky up" a sort of bird cage

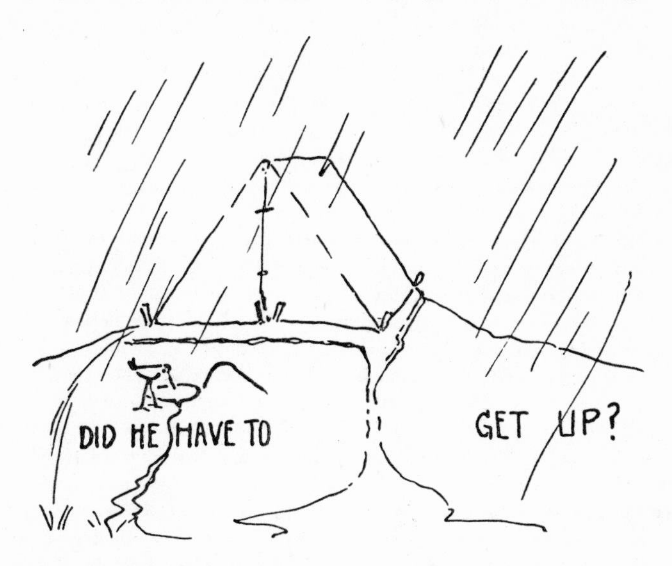

of guava stakes, piled our clothes on it, and built a fire inside this dripping tent of shirts, pants, socks, hippers and undershirts. With this inside and outside heat all were dry in no time—dry enough. Only one undershirt fell through and was burned: The Sachem's. (I didn't need it anyhow.) To resume: Camp Site. Consider all three points: 1. Will the water run away from your tent if it comes on to rain? 2. Will the sun shine on your tent and blanket in the morning? Will it be shady in the heat of the day? And so on. A5, A6, A7: Time-honored weather vane. Set your tent as in the cut, corner to the wind, to avoid flapping. Wind can

Scoops hollow[D6] in gravel after removing sod.[D7] Piles gravel[D8] on sod. Puts paper bag[D9] of charcoal[D10] and shavings[D11] in this hole. Shavings on top.[D12] Lights shavings with one

keep one awake! A8. Clouds! Wind! Squalls! Lightning! Keep away from tall trees and trees with rotten branches. If it looks like rain, trench. Ordinarily you need not dig deep. Merely carve a tiny crack around, enough to lead off a trickle of water. If it comes on a deluge, peel, jump out and fight it. Dig deeper! A9. Camp sites are found by using common sense. A10. See Trespassing, page 164, B1, B2, B3, B4, Pass. B5, B6. Kindness. Frontiersmen make it a religion to tend to animals *first,* their own wants after. Nobody but an idiot would let a dog drink from his private cup. Dogs carry disease. It's the nature of the beast. B7. First Aid! B8, B9, B10. D1, D2. Bad to drink when hot or exhausted. Clogs heart and lungs. If anybody is really down and out, turn to and make him a *stir-a-bout.* To a table-spoon of wetted flour add boiling water and a pinch of salt. Let it really boil for three minutes, stirring merrily. Make your patient take it as hot as he can swallow it and lie down. It should run like molasses. This is not food, but a poultice on his solar plexus—the star place, where all his courage and pep are gathered—like rays of a star. D3. Unships Dirk and Baby. "Unship," "Unpack," "Break Out,"—You must learn these words, for all have different meanings. Unship—take off, let down. Unpack—unstrap, open up. Break out—take out, for use. D4. See page 59. These nails are heavy. Do without them if you care to. Try five-inch wire nails. D5. It is not absolutely necessary to cook near your tent. Find a comfortable place, near water, near wood, etc. But be sure to avoid places near trees, boulders, where wind eddies. The smoke won't stay put.

D6. This is our fire in a plug-hat hole. D7, D8. The gravel or earth on it keeps it moist for *re-sodding!* This was a *play!* But if all campers had re-sodded the holes they dug there would not now be seen so many signs "Trespassers will be prosecuted."

D9, D10, D11, D12, E1, E2, E3. All your practice in outdoor cookery, on a Jack-knife or mess-kit basis, will be easier if you use charcoal. You'll then know what you *want,* in a fire. Try match[E1] (cheers), places bits of charcoal on top of burning shavings, brushes leaves and twigs[E2] away (dumb show) to prevent fire spreading.[E3] (Cheers from the Head Forester.) Ties neckerchief across forehead and washes[E4] his hands. (Cheers[E5] from the nurses of St. Francis' Hospital.) Tells dog to lle down,[E6] on guard.

Cooks his supper with mess-kit.[E7]

Ham and eggs,[E8] bread and jam.[E9]

He sets[E10] his table using neckerchief as table cloth.

charcoal in a hole, lighting only the top. Covered with ashes this will smoulder till you want it again. When you fan up the ashes, up she comes, bright as ever. Hot stuff! No wonder the forester cheered.—How many feet of lumber are ruthlessly burned every year. Some day parts of our wonderful country may look like the Sahara—no trees—no water, and dirty Bedouins, all that are left of us, fleeing from the floods of their ancestors' making. E4. Ties up his face and washes his hands before he cooks! I got this from a famous West Point Captain. It goes too. Do it, *please.* Why? Obvious. E5. Of course they cheered. Microbes! Sweat in my stew? No thank you—not even my own.

E6. Does your dog mind *you?* (Remember this was a show stunt.) I use it to sum up my theory of camping and behavior. E7, E8, E9. All easy. See Chapter I. The huge jar of jam made the big hit. E10. Are you a Bedouin? They eat with their hands out of one pot. Our method isn't flossie or sissy. It's merely comfortable. So *set* your table. Be civilized. F1. All good cooks will smile at this. Scientific! F2, F3. How about it? Did you leave all your *code* behind, or do you take it along? F4. Cowboy practice—ditto Cavalry—ditto Good Sport. F5. By this time water is hot. "No soap for your cups," said Peter, my Indian guide to the Hudson Bay region. (A lot of him is in this book—*ba-leeve-me!*) "Soap for dishes only." Swab with a bunch of grass, or a swabber. F6. With the soapy water! Scientific! F7.

Before he eats he puts pail [F1] on for hot water for his dish washing. He then stands a moment *silent*.[F2] He salutes the Great Spirit [F3] for what he is about to receive, and goes to it, first feeding the *dog*.[F4] (Cheers from the Cowboys.) Washes dishes.[F5] After washing up, he puts out his fire,[F6] resods [F7] the hole, obliterates [F8] all traces of his cooking place,[F9] for, you see, he intends to have his breakfast on the road tomorrow, homeward bound.

He then plants a hickory nut [F10] to grow into a tree, so that there'll be *Hickory* for the next generations of Appledips.[G1]

Unpacks pack.[G2] (Ration Bag or "Baby" is already off.)

Unrolls tent.[G3] Pitches tent [G4] in 1 minute 30 seconds,[G5] using nails as pegs. (These are per-

If only good Americans would! F8. "So the injuns won't find ye" (Fenimore Cooper).

F10. Here, if they had been there and had seen it, Theodore Roosevelt, John Muir, Johnnie Appleseed and Gifford Pinchot: all would have cheered. As it was it didn't get a hand. Nut was too small. Nobody *saw* it. Too bad! Such is life. Try next year again. G1. Appledip evidently thought *way ahead*. G2. "Not until you have cooked," says Stewart Edward White. "You can put up a tent in the dark but camp cookery by stump-of-candle-light is a bore, cook and eat first. G3, G4, G5, G6, G7. Use your tent bag as a pillow. Stuff it with your extra dry shirt, if no hay. Your bag of flour wouldn't be bad—but don't boast about it. G8. It takes clever folding to keep these pegs from jabbing holes in your tent. G9. Cut grass, hay, etc., if you like. Tuck it under the edge of your blanket which must be turned or folded under you even on a hot night. In winter I want three under, three over!

manently attached to the tent.) Spreads ground-cloth [G6] on ground [G7] inside the tent. Spreads blanket on ground-cloth.[G8] Stuffs his pillow.[G9] He now takes off his shoes. Discovers a red spot [G10] on his heel.[H1] Pastes plaster over this place (All Army Captains cheer).[H2] Discovers a hole in stocking. Darns it, using shoe-heel as "darning egg." [H3] (All the mothers cheer!)

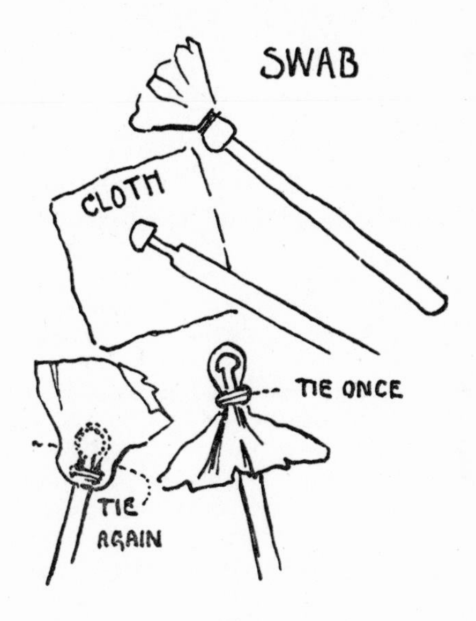

YARN

After a year in Borneo, sleeping on a mat, on a hard wood floor, on the deck of a launch, on the bamboo slats of a "rest house," on the way up those forever long rivers, I at last found myself in a real bed again: Hong Kong Hotel, Suite A. Feather bed. It nearly choked me. Got up. Broke out my old sleeping mat and rattan pillow, slept on the floor. So can you sleep on

Opens a bird book,[H4] and spots a bird.[H5] Notes this down in a log—or journal[H6] of his trip. (William Beebe and all the Teachers at Columbia cheer.) Yawns.[H7] Dog yawns.[H8] Time to turn in (8 P.M.).[H9] Boy retires into his tent leaving dog outside[H10] on guard. [Meanwhile a regular circus was going on. Twenty-five foot tower erected in 11 minutes and telegraph wires laid to top. Signalling. Up hospital tent. Up lean-to's up and down; all kinds of good work by boys. Much cheering.] "Comes the dawn"[J1] as the movies say. Bill Appledip comes out of his tent clad in scarlet[J2] pyjamas; yawns, Salutes[J3] the Rising Sun, stretches[J4] and does his "daily dozen."

a flat, hard place. Camping isn't the Ritz, nor the Hong Kong Hotel, Suite A.

G10. Keep on with the show! Examine your feet. A red spot means a wicked blister usually. H1, H2. Blisters spoil many a tramp. At Plattsburg (1915) when I was Corporal of the 14th Squad, Company I (highest military rank ever attained by me—) the Sergeant "Doctor" said "Let out the water, wash with Germicide soap, dry and plaster." H3. In one show Billy used the very same egg that later went into his fry-pan. (Combined cheers from the mighty throng.) H4, H5, H6. Bird study: names and habits of plants, trees, wild flowers—lovely diversions; opening books whose pages grow stale only when the heart grows cold. Begin young!

. . . H7, H8, H9, H10. You'll need every wink of it—nine hours—This allows for the Hoot Owl scare (time out—15 minutes) the Banshee call (two limbs sawing together in the night wind) and the porcupine that walks right in, bent on eating your shoes. Can you tell the sound of a Katydid from a Tree Frog? And

Spreads his blanket and ground cloth on top of his tent to air in the sun, off the ground. Breaks out a towel,[J5] tooth-brush,[J6] soap[J7]—takes up dog and departs to the swimming hole.[J8] Comes back, hair all wet. Dog's foot has recovered—no more bandage. Appledip disappears into his tent. Comes out dressed.[J9] Combs his hair[J10] using bottom of frying pan as looking

HIS COOKING KIT WAS SHINING BRIGHT

remember—be up at early dawn—earlier the better. J1. How cool the dew on your heels! This is the Kneipp cure; walk around in the dew. You won't catch cold. J2. Scientific! Deer hunters! J3. (All the Persians, Hindoos and Zoroastrians cheered.) They worship the sun!

glass. Empties pillow. Burns rubbish. Rolls blanket in ground cloth. Straps it.[K1] Strikes tent.[K2] Bags it. Folds it. Assembles same with blanket roll. Baby and dirk, and ties up "all snug" with his leather thongs. Inserts poles. Slings[K3] on his pack, mess kit, canteen—Salutes[K4] the Grand Stand and exit William.

J4. Keep on stretching like the cat. Breathe deep and stretch. Arms, legs, lie down and ride a bicycle upside down. Keep it up all your life! (You know what I mean.) Be kind to your body. This is the hour to get rid of all your rubbish—to clean house. J5, J6, J7. Without which no gentleman travels. Carried in the blanket and poncho roll. J8. Or a little later. We won't be exacting. But you are missing something fine—the dawn plunge! J9, J10. Makes a hit annually. The world, when it stops to think, likes the kind of man who bathes, shaves, has nice white teeth, nails. He is *very liable* to be on the square. (While I write this those Bedouins are moving again. The sheik of our village (pronounced "Sheck") has ordered them off. Reason? No code. Too dirty—they mess the whole place up. We have some "B's" in our fair land too—more's the pity! They travel in motors and a trailer and leave a mess behind them.) K1. See the diagrams. K2. Pitch tent: strike tent: fold tent: pack tent. Assemble pack. Strap, tie, sling on, adjust—and away you go. K3. De-lighted! K4. With my best wishes—Aloha!

You would be surprised to know how many men of brains have contributed to this stunt. Here are some: Dan Beard, Charlie Hanks, Horace Kephart, Stewart Edward White, Charlie Smith, Dr. Plummer—besides the number, *legion,* of Boy Scouts whom I have camped with in my time.

Of course nobody will stick to *rules*—not for long. Each man or boy comes to do it *his own way,* elaborates on it, cuts it down. I must tell you, however, that *I think* Billy Appledip's way is about *right.*

So, if you have followed the words (and action) of this "Play" and looked up all the foot-

OFF HE GOES

notes, very patiently, you can do it, *camp,* just like "our hero."

CHAPTER V

ACCIDENTS

First aid does not mean last aid—though some of the boy-first-aid I have seen, applied by loving and willing hands, might well have been called *very last aid.* Boys are apt to pick out some one thing in a lecture and forget the context—what came before—and after—and so do some silly thing.

When a boy is "apparently drowned"—has been under water from 5 to 15 minutes, *even 30 minutes,*—the Army, Navy, Red Cross, Boy Scouts—nearly every First Aid Society applies what is called Shaeffer's Prone Method—"Face down, shove him in the small of the back." One of the ways of making newly born babies first breathe and also half-drowned people, is to give them a good hard *spank.* One night my turn came to examine a class in First Aid before some ladies and gentlemen and the class was made up of some small boys. "When a lady faints what do you do?" (The answer is: *Lay her out flat on her back, no pillow.*) I asked this question of a red-haired, freckled boy who seemed to know the answer. So I said—"Yes, Willie?"

"Lay her flat on her face and spank her," says he. Instead of leaving the room all the ladies nodded approval—and Willie was a hero.

You mustn't mix things up.

My idea of First Aid is: *Begin Before You NEED It!* And stop your pal from doing foolish things with fire, water, axes, knives, etc.

But things do happen, even to *scientific* campers, and we will discuss the matter first for *Jack-knifers.* What do you do when the doctor and the drug store are miles and miles away? What can you do with nothing but a Jack-knife?—And no doctor?

Pain is a warning.

Nature's big remedy is rest.

Get out of harm's way. Don't go on injuring the patient by tossing him about. Splint broken bones; keep warm or cool, as your common-sense tells you is the thing to do. Sometimes hot canteen or heated stones (not too hot to rest against your own cheek), blankets; shade sometimes—sometimes cool water—sometimes warm. And having done your best—BRING A DOCTOR.

Except in a drowning scare. Here you lose no time—*not one second.* Slam your insensible pal on his face. Don't stop to "arrange him" but go to work pressing down, firmly but gently, every five seconds, on his lower spine just below his "floating ribs" with your two spread out hands. Make him snore and gurgle every five seconds. Say "Out goes the water—In comes the air." Practice this with a timepiece. If you can get help keep your patient warm, his mouth clear—and keep up the pumping,—which sucks in air and drives it out again—for *hours* and *hours.*

The record, so the Whale tells me, is *life* after twenty-five minutes under water. So keep it up! The "nearly drowned" sometimes breathe once or twice and then stop. Go at 'em again. Never say die. Send for the up-to-date bulletin of the Red Cross. *

Big Cuts and Bleeding.

Again you must not wait to bring a doctor. Even a boy should know that arteries squirt jets of bright scarlet blood, and that most of the big ones run along opposite the seams in your trousers and sleeves. A tourniquet is a string, your lanyard, tied above the cut artery with a piece of wood pressing and squeezing the blood-tube *against a bone.* You *keep cool,* and find the artery by pressing down here and there where you think the artery is, until the spurt stops. Then you bind the cut with a roll of bandage,

* Wilbert E. Longfellow, Red Cross—L. S. C.

all snug. No time to wash the place—the blood itself is a prime cleanser and a good doctor will fix that up later.

Tourniquets are very dangerous. When the arm or leg aches you let out the tourniquet or you may kill the limb.

All this is usually taught in our American schools. LEARN IT!

Broken Bones.

Splints and bandages.

Keep the splinters of bone from cutting arteries.

Don't move him until you have given up all hope (by *telephone* first—or by stopping a motor or a cart) of getting a doctor to *come to the place.* Put up a strong fight to get him. That's the safest *first aid.*

Sprains.

A bad sprain often means a broken ankle. That old saw of "Walk it off" is BUNK. Like "rubbing with liniment" or "arnica"—or "castor oil" (for stomach ache). I traveled a whole year in Borneo with two prime good doctors and they blew off steam sometimes on "Medical Bunk." It's *circulation* you want for sprains—and soap-suds is a fair liniment. Gentle massage does the work. Sprains are bad, of course, but hot water and gentle stroking is the last word. And go home—crawl to a road and wait for help! As for "belly-ache"—drink hot water and don't eat too much next time.

Ptomaine Poisoning. Use an emetic!

Yarn No. 6

Hal Sayre was lone-camping in the mountains of Wyoming. With a horse and pack-mule.

For supper he had a tin of Pork and Beans, some bread and butter and tea. He put on a kettle of water for his dishes and was enjoying the scene and a pipe—when he suddenly felt dizzy and very sick. In a few minutes he was in such agony that he thought he was dying. He crawled to the kettle and wrapped himself around it. That eased the pain some. Then he drank little by little the whole kettle of warm water. Up it came at the second quart. He had been poisoned by bad beans and this emetic—warm water—made him throw up. As it was, when some prospectors found him next day, he was too sick to ride his bronco—had to be toted tied behind one of his rescuers.

The hot water emetic! A little mustard (if you have it) makes it work quicker. Clean house!

Constipation. Jack-knifers must look out for this condition.

The horrible stuff called "Castor Oil" was the

terror of my boyhood. My Mother administered it instead of a strapping, *usually,* and I always begged for the strap or hair brush. I preferred them. Now we can take a perfectly tasteless mineral oil which goes under various names. Its action is *mechanical.* You will feel lots better when out camping, if you use this oil sparingly. A very little is enough—say a teaspoonful before breakfast.

Don't be careless about this! The excitement, the labor, the change in daily conditions of "board" and "lodging," when out camping, sometimes work havoc with one's insides. You must correct this, when necessary, without pills. Mineral Oil, refined, is the sure way.

Little Cuts. No Jack-knifer should ever cut himself! But if you do, bind yourself up snugly and keep quiet and cool. Old Lady Nature staunches ordinary cuts, gashes even, in her own way. She lets the blood curdle or clot and if you don't fuss with it it will stop even though you lose what seems a lot of blood. One does not always wash a bad cut—the blood itself is a good cleanser, for a little while. *But go home.*

"First Aid—one of the best—is the *telephone.*" Don't run three miles for a doctor when a telephone is nearer.

Snake-bite! If you are camping about in snake country you must read up on the subject.

I pass here (no snakes in Hawaii!) but I have heard this on the best authority.

Northern rattlesnakes are not as poisonous as those in the Southern latitudes. A "venom serum" is sold now-a-days in snake-infested country and one must know how to use a hypodermic needle—and all that.

Snakes go to bed at twilight—so unroll your blankets after dark, and avoid a strange bedfellow. Putting hair rope around a sleeping bag or tent, on the theory that a snake will not crawl over it, has been exploded. They *will* cross it.

The ancient way to treat a snake bite was to poison the patient with alcohol—whiskey—but that is exactly the wrong thing to do. The books say: Don't stop to kill the snake! Don't suck the wound. Jab around the bitten place (which shows two deep holes and marks of small, harmless teeth) with your knife. Squeeze out the blood, which carries away some of the poison—tie the limb, usually the leg, above the wound. Rub crystals of Permanganate of Potassium into these cuts. When the limb aches, ease off a little. This lets the venom into your circulation in small doses only.

Snakes, all but the Lance Snake of the Liu Kiu Islands, which *hunts* for you, are usually anxious to get out of a man's way. Help out by being just as anxious to keep clear of them.

The Enemy! Discomfort!

Damp blankets, no rubber sheet, spoiled food, under-cooked food, impure water, dirty dishes, mad dogs, poisonous snakes, falling down a well, blowing up with gasoline, breaking legs, arms, shooting your head off and using carbolic acid instead of maple syrup—these are some of the ways that you might be "bumped off" while on the desert island. As Jack London said—"It is *so* easy." Study all these awful things, therefore, and determine to scrape by. More boys have been killed by hiking too far and too fast—swimming when over-heated—sleeping in a wet blanket or on damp ground than ever were shot or bitten to death by snakes, lions, or elephants.

Bad Water

The easiest way to spoil a week-end on Robinson Crusoe's Islet is to drink water out of a ditch, especially when hot. The wild men of the Congo can stand it, they say, but not a mother's hope. So use your body *right*. It isn't a bit smart to bungle an expedition—not so much on your own account—for you deserve to get a wallop for silly work—but for the other fellow: your pal, or pals, who must carry you home, or your home-staying pals, father and mother. And other fathers and mothers who hear about you, and *their* son, who wanted to learn *self-reliance* (which has never yet been taught—especially out of a book. You must try it out yourself). Your failure hurts everybody.

Overdoing It

Jack-knifers loathe the Smart Aleck who says "Ah, there! You've got everything but a rat trap! Looka me—I sleep on the ground like a man." At 45, when he is needed by a wife and six children, ten to one he has rheumatism or dyspepsia or something—and is cross at breakfast. It's a sure sign. And those lusty, long-distance hikers who could never be made to say they were tired and would urge the pale but plucky "other fellow" (who had a blistered heel and an empty stomach) to "just one more mile"—where are they now? In my case, and I knew a lot of them, and am now more than a half-a-century on deck and still going strong (10 miles is my limit—six is better fun) this ilk have mostly all died off—leaving the green glades of earth for another generation.

Be sure your plans and your outfit are safe and sane like Billy Appledip's!

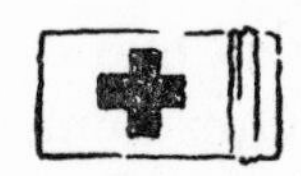

A Suggested First Aid Kit

One foot of half-inch adhesive tape. rolled.
A one-inch bandage.
A "base-ball" wad of absorbent cotton.
In small bottles—Homeopathic sort:

Bicarbonate of soda—for bad burns.

Synol Soap. Liquid for washing cuts and sores, blisters, etc.

Mercurochrome.

Permanganate (for foul water and snake-bite) or

Snake venom with hypodermic needle—ready to use.

(Foolish to carry—except in special

places where boys must be properly trained for a snake-bite.)

Nujol—three doses.

Boracic salve—in a tube.

This will all pack in a screw-top mailing tube. This kit is stowed in the "Baby," where you can get at it without unstrapping your pack-roll.

José (Ho-Zay)

I had a great pal once, a "Chamorro" boy, whose mother handed him over into my care for "twenty years." Our contract was—First: I would feed, clothe, and educate him. On the other hand this small boy engaged himself to serve *me*. "Three days' journey a-foot, three nights without sleep" was the top limit of service. Anything short of this was to be done cheerfully! I hired him at zero per year and never have I seen or heard of a more faithful servant. Servant? I mean *boss*—for he became my manager, butler, waiter, valet—all but cook. His name was José de Castro y Wilson—and he was descended from noble Spaniards, a few years back.

I presented him to my young bride one day as a wedding present, whereupon, very logically, he turned all his attention to the new head of the house, and listened to me, thenceforward, but always rebutted my orders with "Missis Wilder, he say *no.*"

Shall I tell you how the French cook, angry because José caught her stealing sugar, called him a *slave?* How José asked me if this was true? How I denied it, and went into the kitchen and said "Here are your wages to date, José"? Two years' wages! 1000 francs! (Nana's face was a study! Silence—big silence!) How José spent the larger part of this on a present to his dear mother in Guam?

I may as well tell you the story. That little untutored savage blew in 700 francs on *sardines.* It made a crate nearly as big as our piano and took six men to hoist it up to my studio (in Paris). There it stayed until I found by much wasted endeavor, that nothing but U. S. Warships were touching at Guam, and a crate of sardines was out of the question. So we started to eat them. Old Nana was a fine cook. We had sardines, cold. Sardines with tomato sauce. Sardine loaf; Sardine Bullets; Sardine à la Poulette, Sardine Marny, Sardines . . . wait! By that time, and to this day a sardine gives me a pain.

Poor José! One day in France, where he daily rode my bicycle around the little village of St. Marguerite, he took a header and *scraped his knee.* This happened in front of a stable and a French quack doctor dressed it. This man failed to treat this very small scraped place *with an antiseptic.* Just washed it with water. No iodine, no anything. Poor José . . . lock-jaw set in. He died . . . and is buried at St. Nazaire—where afterwards, in the World War, so many of our men found a resting place. Look out for stables.

Listen then. *Do it yourself* . . . and right away. Alcohol and water, cologne, bay rum, . . . wipe a wound with *anything* that hurts (at a pinch) and tell the doctor at once, when you get home. Nowadays, they inject a Serum. It doesn't hurt. Have it done for luck.

In the nice clean woods there is nothing to fear. But *stables*—look out.

Burns. The worst accidents are not apt to *hurt.* When a steam pipe, on a Sago steamer, off Labuan, in 1887, blew out and burned the engineer, we were all comforted to hear him say "I'm all right, me lads. It does'na pain me." But the ship's doctor asked, "Where does your wife live, Scotty? Send her the orders." He died the next morning.

Shock

When you hear somebody howling he isn't usually badly injured. It is the pale-faced, blinky, cold-sweaty patients that are really hurt. They are suffering from *shock* and the treatment is rest and a hot-water bottle, warm covers—and a warm drink.

Guns vs. Boys

One of my young, deer-hunting pals, years ago, was accidentally shot in the knee. His three companions, who had never heard of *first aid,* bandaged him up with their shirts and *put him on a horse*. He bled all the way home! Ten miles! And died, of course, poor little fellow. Had these distracted boys kept him still, leg elevated, taking turns to hold the artery flat—and brought him an expert to tie it—he might have pulled through and been alive to-day.

Once More! Prevent!

Arteries! Bright blood that *spurts!* Hold your finger on the place, until, by feeling around, you can stop it. Put a wad of clean cotton on it, bind it snugly . . . but not too tight. Oh, what's the use? These accidents are very rare indeed. They will be rarer still if you boys *look ahead,* and *avert, prevent* and avoid them.

Carrying in a Litter

When the patient is fixed up, *and can be carried.*

When he must be moved we make a litter.

Bags, sacks, coats, blankets, pinned sheets. There are all sorts. Be sure the litter is long enough. Try grape-vines, a window shutter, a door or a wide board!

Yarn No. 7

One night I camped with fifteen boys at a lovely place called *Waimano,* on Oahu, in Hawaii. Our camp was scientific, warm, mosquito proof, sheltered—and showed all the marks of expert work: racks for provisions, clothes drying "wicky-up," fire holes—everything. In the night a hideous groan came from the tent No. 7, of the "Bulls." "What's up, Whang?" Whang, a Chinese-American, showed me where he had, in his sleep, kicked against his opened jack-knife. He seemed to have punctured his knee cap for it had a tiny cut and was bluish. No blood. Shock? No shock. His Number One Bull and I (everybody else was fast asleep), found a fire-hole still smouldering at 3 A. M., heated water, wet a "compress" with it, plus a drop or two of "Lysol," good antiseptic, and returned to Bull Seven, who was now asleep. We deftly turned down the blankets and gently moved his leg. It was quite limber. Then we placed the hot compress on his knee cap. A piercing yell from Whang roused the whole camp. "Sow *Kwa!* Sow *fing!*" howled Whang. (Maybe it was a little too hot!) The Boar One, The Owl One, and Bulls, Boars and Owls came pouring forth with multi-colored lights, sputtering candles, torches . . . while Whang *groaned.*

"If the knee is stiff at day break, we must carry him home," said I, gravely. Bull One, Boar One, Owl One, with their "Threes" (First Aiders) will make a *litter. If the knee is stiff.*" *Chorus.* "Let's do it now!" Let's carry him!" "Let's. . . ."

The Old Man: "Enough, varmints. Go back to bed." Morning dawned—I mean "Came the dawn" in Waimano! In the garden of Eden. Wild ducks flew down from the fresh swimming pools, from miles up the gorge. The Ohia trees were bent with luscious, red mountain-apples—and the singing brook called the faithful to the morning plunge. All nature rejoiced in four flats. All but Whang. After his night's rest I found his knee quite rigid. "Will they carry me?" asked he. "Of course! Wounded, women, and children are always carried by the brave."

Boys, boys, boys! Aren't they interesting creatures? Training boys, I had found, in middle-age, gave me as much fun as horse-racing, money making, or golf . . . and was better exercise.

Whang was a good boy but he had become mesmerized. He really thought his knee was stiff. Well, we made the litter. (See diagram, p. 128.)

We carried Whang four miles. Remember this: Carry a living man *head foremost*. A corpse goes feet foremost, on the flats. When you come to a wall, or a fence, operate as given below.

We did all the things we knew to be "scientific." We passed him over barbed wire, through streams, up hill, down dale. Four miles, down

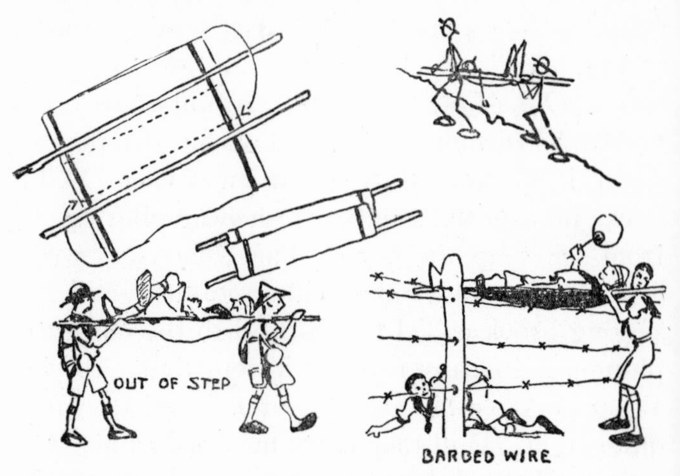

HOW YOU MAKE AND MANAGE LITTERS

hill and up. Relayed by Bulls, Boars, and Owls, who fought for their turns for a mile, and then became *less anxious* to carry Whang—we got him to the railway and on the train. To his oriental mother went flying Bull One (Patrol Leader of the Bull Patrol) to forestall any "shock" on her side. We need not have worried.

"I look," tersely said this excellent Chinese mother. The "compress," scientifically tied on with a neckerchief, now came off. Whang's mother saw no wounds, no blood, even the blue spot had disappeared.

"Sow Kwa! Sow FING-GWA!" Grabbing the "injured" leg she pumped it up and down!

"Sow *Kwa*" . . . she shouted. The dazed Whang arose and walked.

Outside, the Old Man (that's me) addressed the surviving Bulls, Boars and Owls:

"Imagination plays us many tricks, oh, my children." *Chorus*. "Duck him in the river." "Put him through the gauntlet."

The Old Man. Silence. You have learned how to carry a badly wounded man. (Laughter!) The experience, I hope, has been valuable. But since you have missed a whole day of camping and all those mountain-apples (groans) we will all go to witness the big base-ball game between *Kamehameha School* and *Punahou College*." (Cheers!) Go home and change your clothes."

At the game was the erstwhile stricken Whang —but he had paid for his own ticket. Boys are wonderful!

CHAPTER VI

EVERY OLD THING

It was a man called Joseph Knowles, who on a bet, let himself be set down in a Maine forest, *naked,* and, according to the papers, came out of the woods three months later, wearing bear-skin clothes, fox-skin cap, and a well-fed smile, having lived on the land all that time without even a jack-knife. Fire, game, skins, food! A good yarn!

THREE-MAN FIRE-DRILL AT NIAH

The very Prince of Jack-knifers!

It's when you have nothing to work with that brains begin to count.

Fire Without Matches, Flint or Steel. What can we do for a nice fire when all the matches are gone? If it is cold and wet you are in a bad scrape. Better chew your belt and hike for home. But what if you MUST HAVE A FIRE? Somebody's very life may depend on it! And it has been done—fire without matches, in the wet, too!

Fire

I first made fire without matches, *getting ready,* with two pieces of California Red Wood (*Semper virens*) common on the coast. I then

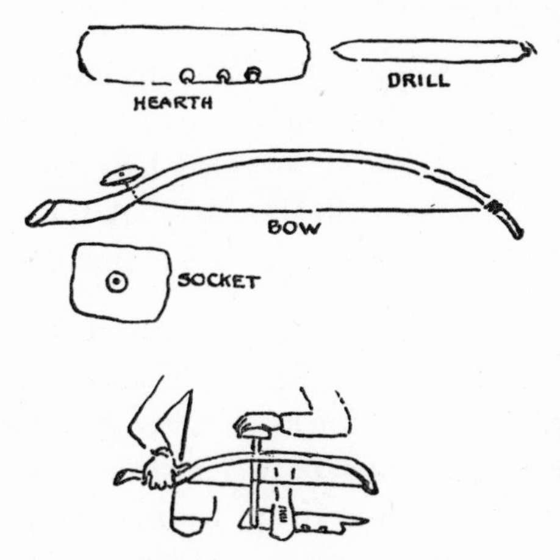

made it, over and over, with South Sea Purau or Hau and a "drill" of hard wood called Alahee. Harder work! Red Wood for me! This is the trick. Dry wood *hearth,* drill, bow, socket and thong. Tinder, shavings . . . as in the illustrations.

Hearth. Must be of wood containing no resin,

such as Red Wood, Cedar, Sugar Pine, Hau,—not a hard nor very soft wood. Roughly cut a fire-pit with a notch and a hole as in diagram.

Drill. A spindle one span long, about 3/4 inch around pointed at both ends.

The Bow. A curved branch—3-span long, stiffish.

The Socket. A chip of wood with a greased hole for your drill.

A Thong. Your leather shoe-lacing or a longer thong. Cut up a boot or a shoe. Hard luck if you have to use string or braided hair from one of the un-bobbed girls in the party. A torn up shirt, braided four-ply and waxed—might do.

Tinder. In the Pacific rotten *wiliwili* (Bot. name *erythrina monosperma,* Gaud) dry coconut husks and various barks of trees (found by experiment) pounded between stones. Try *cedar bark*—used by American Indians. A shredded cotton rag was once used in my presence. Pounded Buffalo chips, droppings of Cattle, Camels, etc. *Try everything,* for the fun of it,—for good tinder is the key to fire by friction.

Pitfalls. The drill when spinning back-and-forth in the fire-pit, must not rattle or wobble. Never touch fire-pit or fire-end of drill with fingers. The oil from your skin delays ignition. Hold your hearth down hard with left-foot . . . your left forearm against the left shin. Not too much slack in your thong—and make it go smoothly. When smoke from the drill is heavy you will find a little pile of burning sawdust under the notch. This must have air. Feed this spark with more of your fine sawdust and when burning like the end of a cigarette (as smoked by gun-men and others) roll this into your tinder and fan it with your hand, at first, then blow gently, then harder and lo! A blaze! The shivering orphans are saved! You light your fire of day[1] tooth-picks and shavings, then you add damp shavings, then damp chips, then your wet wood and the day is saved. Supper at six. Everybody happy!

Yarn No. 8

In Borneo, 1897, I offered a silver dollar as prize for the best *fire-by-friction* and there were ten entries. (It was on the banks of the Niah River, Sarawak, and we had instituted some games to while away the steam-heat hours.) In a rusty note-book, now riddled by book-worms, I can still decipher the outlandish names of the

[1] The inside of a soaking branch is usually dry. Cut off the wet outside and shave the dry inside very thin.

contestants, and sketches of the implements used. Olong Kiat, Kenya Tribe; one "Poo-nan," (the real "wild man-o-Borneo," a ferocious-looking half-naked savage from the jungle); Liang, Long Patah Tribe; a man of the Malanau Tribe; Madang, Imang, Kenya men from away up the Baram River; Padong, an "Undup"; Jallong, a Ballau; Paha, a Miri-man. The Punan was Sako, and so on. All were to make their fire-making machines on the spot, tinder from the near-by jungle, etc. Time limit one hour. They all made it within the set time, the wild man walking off with the dollar, for when he got at it he had fire in forty seconds! This is how Sako did it.

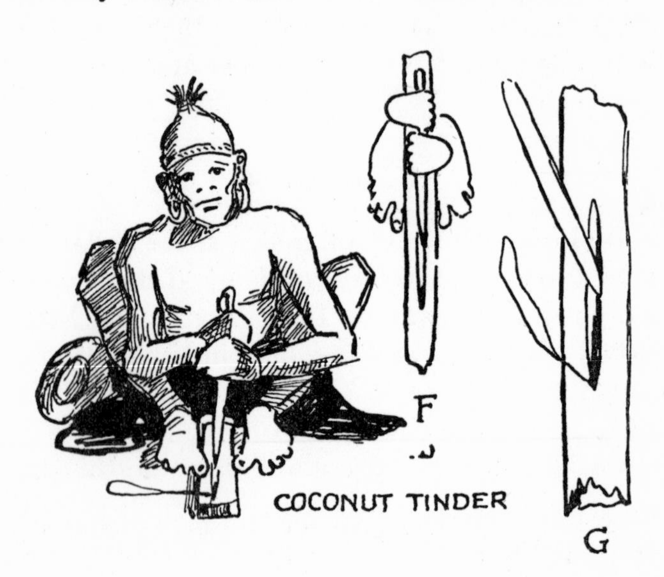

Squatting, he held his *hearth* between his strong "prehensile" big toes. He then violently rubbed on it—with another stick, using both hands—and at the far end of a smoking groove that shortly appeared, there started a spark. He blew on this, tossed it into some tinder (from a sort of fern, so they told me) and waved it in the air! This burst into flame! Time 40 seconds! (The U. S. record is 15 seconds, with a drill.)

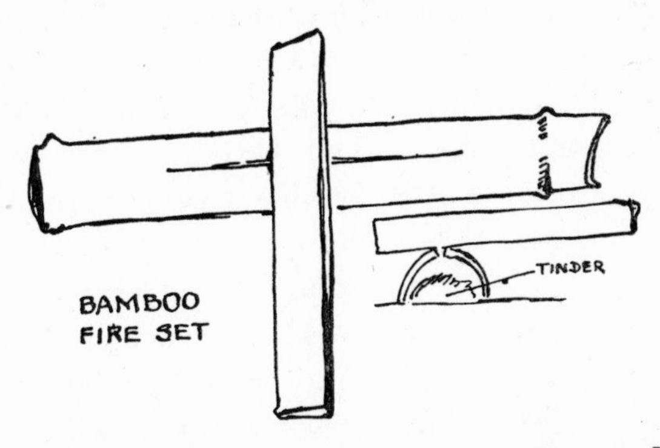

Meanwhile another man did it thus: He used dry bamboo, one split, the other fashioned like a knife and used as a saw. One minute! You may see a bamboo fire-set, like this one in the New York Museum of Natural History—for the Filipinos make fire this way—in a few seconds,—so do the Chinese in the Upper Yangtse, and others.

Try this with two pieces of cedar or red-wood, together, with saw of the same material! It may *never yet have been done!* It ought to work!

But to continue: The Poonan, on being presented with a silver dollar disappeared. We thought we had lost him. Not at all—he came back with some "Dammar gum" like tar, and a sliver of *flint*—I watched him as he affixed this pointed stone to the end of a stick with the gum, which he heated over a few coals. Then he proceeded to drill a hole in the dollar by simply twirling this "drill" between his hands! Then he hung the prize around his neck on a string. Oh, my wild Poonan! How I could forever have watched you work! He was a Jack-knifer without any code—not our code. He had been taught to fear anything strange, like a wild animal, and his motto was "when in doubt, *kill.*" He lived in a tree-hut, like a monkey, and carried a short blow gun, or "pea-shooter" in which he used a deadly poisoned dart. Another of our "Olympic Games" (for another silver dollar) was won by the man named Liang, of the Long Patah tribe. The target was a hard-boiled pheasant's egg peeled and stuck up in a cleft-stick at a range of fifty feet.

Of ten contestants only one man missed it! They riddled a dozen eggs—and Sako the Punan (that's the way to spell it) lost out by one point. But Liang was mature and cool, *steady.* The Punan was younger and over-anxious—and surrounded by strange people, white men who practised magic, and he was jumpy! I was considered a witch-man who made spirit images with a black box and a crystal eye—camera! He always watched me with scared eyes. [Look up Sarawak, Borneo, on a map, and with your finger follow up the River Niah to a cross where you will see the words "Mammoth Caves"—that's the place! It was here I saw rice cooked in a pitcher-plant and in nodes of bamboo—and this brings me to another chapter.]

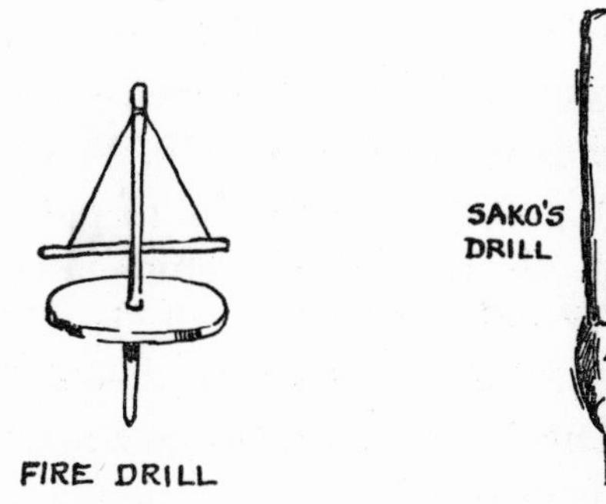

Yankee Boys—Americans—are spoiled when it comes to food. They want a lot and a big variety. But the Dutch—Hollanders—are happy with cheese and bread. Germans will go in for a chunk of black bread and an onion and never grumble. Japanese—ball of cold rice and a pickled plum, and so on.

What if you want something light? To use on the march? Something light to carry in a bag that you can nibble on when hungry? The Red Man carried parched wheat or corn. It was boiled first, then dried, then roasted. A handful and a swallow of water was a meal. On it the Indian runner could travel for months—helped out with a buffalo once in a while, I hope.

Here is another. Grape-nuts, currants and sugar, mixed. In Hawaii: Dried squid and *paiae,* or pounded taro—what the Kanakas love and we old stagers could live on forever. The squid, or octopus, is salted and dried hard in the sun, then broiled over coals. This makes it soft—delicious! The taro root is steamed, scraped, and pounded to a hard sort of mashed potato. When you are hungry you gouge out a fist-ful of *paiae,* wrench off, or cut off a slice of squid—and oh my! Broiled? Wonderful! Raw, it is tough—but good. Like eating a shoe with a slab of half-dried mucilage. One must be a South Sea man to really adore this combination.

"On a clothes line in the sun

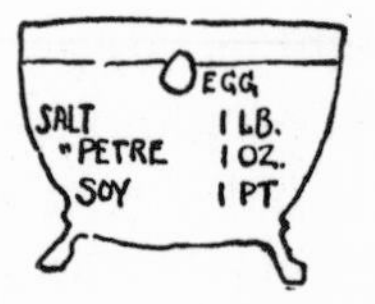

Rope or Jerky

Venison or Beef dried in strips. Most sustaining and handy to eat. While on the march you cut off a junk and chew on it. Good for your teeth! Here is old Rawhide Ben's recipe for Jerky. Best ever! Cut a tender piece of meat into long strips the size of your thumb and soak it overnight in salt with some salt-petre and a sprinkling of soy. (See soy.) This "brine" must just float a fresh egg. (Jack-knifery Desert Island Hydrometer!)

Next day hang it up to dry on a clothes line in the sun. Now boil down the salty red liquor that has oozed from the beef to one-half; a sort of soup. Take in your Jerky, off the line, at sunset, and stow it in a dry place, *away from the dogs* and covered from flies. Next day, when the sun is up, dip your Jerky in the soup again and hang it up once more. Dry it until it is *hard*—then put it in a wide-lipped bottle for future use. Good for stews or broiled or just raw.

Sometimes a choice piece of beef is left over. Cooking it will keep it awhile but salting it down will keep it a month. On a large scale for a lot of people, your "brine" should float an egg, but in your case you will not have enough liquid to test it thus. Experience is the best teacher—Not too salty!

Sea-going Food. Cooking in a boat is done in a box filled almost full with sand. An old drip-pan may be used as a hearth for your fire and with a grill on top you can cook almost anything. Charcoal preferred as fuel, but any kind in a pinch.

CHAPTER VII

Sea-going Menus

Bubble-and-squeak is a stew made of salt-pork, cut into dice and fried down. Then sliced cabbage is fried in the grease. Then hard-tack is crumbled into it, with water, and some Worcestershire Sauce, and canned milk and water, added slowly. This is *said* to cure seasickness—you live or die—you perhaps won't care which.

Lobscouse. Four pilot biscuits crushed. Juice from a can of Alaska Salmon, thicken over a slow fire with the crackers and some milk, canned of course, add 1 teaspoon of A1, Worcestershire or Soy, salt and paprika; mix in the solid salmon and serve hot. A good, quick, cheap dish. (Had this at Bolabola and liked it.)

Chowder. Make this ashore where there is plenty of room. Fry down, salt pork-scraps to the crisp. In same fat fry onions a golden brown. Cut your cleaned fish into handsome cubes, the size of a dollar. Stow these aside. The tails, heads, "small fry" and the bones of the big fish are now boiled with very little water in one pot. Some peeled potatoes in another—until 3/4 done.

Now fill pot No. 1 in which you fried your pork and boiled your onions and then "bones," with a mixture of condensed milk, 1 part, to water plus the bone-soup nicely strained 1½. Add your potatoes. When the milk is just about to boil, add your dollar junks of fish. Boil gently until fish is "set." Then add crushed pilot bread and ladle it out to the hungry crew.

[1. Scraps to cover the bottom of the pot.
2. Onions to make a good layer atop these. (Fry to a nice golden brown. Watch out!)
3. Potatoes to cover this last layer, placed side by side, cut into dice the size of a walnut.
4. Fish to make two layers on top the spuds.
5. Milk-1, "soup"-and-water 1½—to fill the pot ¾ full.]

Bigger the crew, bigger the pot.

Of course a few oysters, clams, lobster will go into this, but chowder is *chowder* and a mixture becomes ***NEAR BOUILLABAISSE,*** a fish stew poured over fresh slices of bread.

Clean all the smaller fish, boil them with the bones and heads of your big fish until you have a rich fish soup, seasoned with Thyme, Rosemary salt, pepper. Cut your big fish into golf-ball pieces and when you have carefully strained the soup, drop them in. Not too long! Just long enough to set the flesh. Adding fried onions, tomatoes and celery to the soup is my fancy . . . and a pinch of saffron to turn it a golden yellow.

Baccalau. Soak slabs of salt cod. Then boil awhile. Pour off this water and boil again . . . slow . . . for hours, until very tender. Then add peeled onions, potatoes, tomatoes and a bell pepper. Taste for salt. Add herbs. This awful dish is beloved by the Basques in the Bay of Biscay and like the Chili Con Carne of the Cowboys, a pot of it is kept going night and day . . . with additions. Poured over toast it isn't so bad.

Starvation Foods

The Hawaiians say "I ka wa wi ai ka ki" (in time of famine eat the ki). It is good to know the pot herbs and the edibles of your own section of the world. In Hawaii are 41 varieties of wild foods, a list of which I sent to the Botanical Museum at Harvard long ago. Fronds of various ferns, several nuts, roots, seaweeds, to say nothing of sea food . . . limpets, crabs, and so on, which most of us White Kanakas know where to find and how to prepare. Some will knock you out if you are not taught to prepare them by pounding, washing, baking.

Here is a list of some foods growing wild in the Sierra Nevadas, California, given me by the

"Queen of the Yosemite." I asked her what a man could live on, maintain life on, in those to me gigantic spaces. If I remember them they were fish, game, acorns, pine-nuts, grass-hoppers, larvae in dead wood, earth-worms, wild onions, camass ESCULENTA (one kind is poisonous) and BRODEA. All this was interesting, for one of my father's stories was of a man who had starved to death in the mountains near Natchez-under-the-hill. With all that to live on!

Every state in the Union has its own particular sort of Starvation Grub. I couldn't starve on my Desert Island and you, on yours, should begin to study your own particular case. The worst of it is we are always apt to be thousands of miles from home when the big adventure comes.

Emergency Coffee

I, once, in my dreams, wondered if water would boil in a bottle. But would it? Let us now, as I did, emulate Lord Bacon, greatest genius of our era, whose mind has still to be matched by any English speaking man, in my opinion, to this date. He believed in *experimentation.* "Try it out," said Bacon. Test your "book-theories," your "supposed facts," by trying it out. But be scientific and don't make the same mistake twice. That's the "New Learning." Bacon started it about Mayflower time—up to then people usually followed the book as blind as bats. In the Beaux Arts School, in France, the professors give out "Projects" or "Problems," and it is up to the student to solve them. I believe in sucking honey from all the flowers—leaving the poison for spiders. Let's try a "Project" à l'école des Beaux Arts!

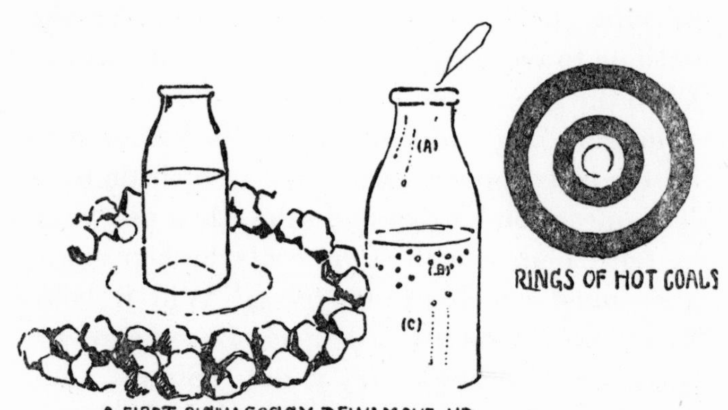

A. FIRST SIGN: FOGGY DEW: MOVE UP.
B. SECOND SIGN: UNDER WATER BUBBLES: MOVE UP.
C. BOILING: NOW THE COFFEE.

Given a case—of some people—one very much exhausted, lost in the mountains or "cut off by a flood" (Our Desert Island). Somebody *must* have a cup of hot coffee, that is vitally necessary. The only available vessel is a quart milk bottle (Of course, coffee, sugar, and cream, *luckily*.) How would you make the coffee? Now the books say, and most people believe, that fire cracks a milk bottle and that one cannot possibly boil coffee in one. But is that *so?*

Procedure. Wash the bottle. Start a bed of *coals,* in a very sheltered place. Stand your bottle, half full of good water, on a dry, flat spot of earth. Make a fire-ring of half-spent coals about a ½ span from the base of your bottle. When the glass is warm and steam congeals in the upper, cold neck, move your coals nearer and continue to edge up to about three inches away. When the glass is hot to the touch and the steam no longer *condenses,* but begins to escape and wet the leaf-stopper, and a myriad of little bubbles appears on bottom and sides, then pile your fire-fence higher, with newer coals, broken small. Coals must not touch the glass! Will it boil? Without breaking? Be a Francis Bacon and *see.* Never mind the book—*try it out.* (Simply adding your coffee and sugar, letting it boil a little, then raking your fire away—that's all!) The beautiful blonde is saved! Can't you hear her say —"Oh, Mr. Appledip, how fortunate we were to have had you here to-day!" When I first did this trick at Murray Bay on the St. Lawrence a proud and scornful New Yorker, all dressed up, walked by. "What are you doing?" he asked. "Saving a beautiful—I mean boiling water in an old beer bottle." "Well," said he, very scornfully indeed. . . . "When you've *done* it what earthly *good* is it?" And passed scornfully and proudly on his unsympathetic way. How many thousands of bottles are going to be cracked hereafter, by my young readers, I know not, but whoever does the trick may drop me a line or postal ("Aloha Tower," Honolulu) and be enrolled in the Milk-bottle Coffee Club.

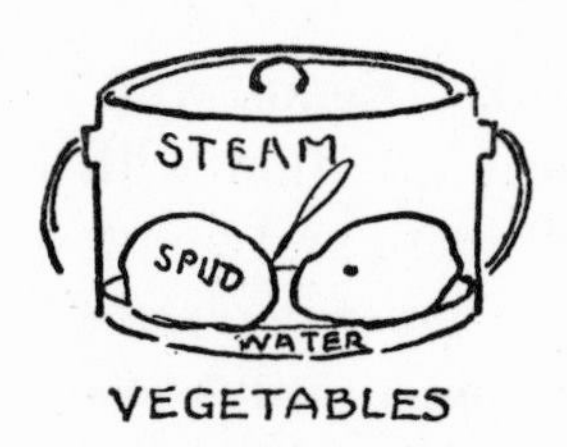

VEGETABLES

Vegetables. If you have a top to your pail use only a little water and "steam" your vegetables. In the Imu, if you suspect the ground to be very dry and want your vegetables juicy, soak them in water for an hour before, and just as you cover the hole, pour a handful of water through a hole in the top. It is seldom necessary.

CHAPTER VIII

Miscellaneous

Butchery. Make friends with a good butcher. Discuss the meat question with him. They are usually nice, fat men, and know what is best for the money. But what *if* you must kill, skin, clean and cut up your own meat? We Honolulu boys of 1880 all learned how! By looking on!

There was a sort of gallows in the little village with a long name; ULUPALAKUA. Two cowboys or PANIOLO (for our "cowboys" are the historically first in this country—taught by Mexicans—Paniolo-españiolos—120 years ago), would drag down from the hills a ferociously wild bull, held hard by the horns with two stout raw-hide lassos, and proceed to tie him to a tree. We kids would line the high fence and watch this doomed beast paw the ground and bellow. How his eyes would glare! This was to cool him off—for meat, fish, fowl, is not good if it dies hot with rage or exertion! Kill them quick and mercifully! (Fish especially.) When they are happy. Or let 'em cool. Then, with a long sharp knife—there!

I simply can't stand it! Go to the butcher and buy your meat.

An army cook once told us all about beef—the various cuts and so forth by a series of antics which he performed on himself.

"Here's yo' calves' brains," tapping his head. "Sweetbreads, here, near de Adam's Apple. Rib Roast here—where yo' saddle come on a mule."

Herd Cookery

By this I mean cookery on a big scale in time of trouble.

The men may be wanted on some larger job so it might be up to the boys to handle the Cuisine. Once you know the kabob and the twister, nobody need go hungry for long . . . for a little instruction will do wonders.

Beef, mutton, bread and coffee . . . you should be able to handle these things on a big scale. Keep your nerve, that's all!

Notes. Australian Dampers can be made up to ten pounds.

Coffee can be made in ordinary buckets. Full sized Imus can be covered with matting, carpets, canvas, sheets and earth. Better to over cook than under and be sure the Imu is not ruined by somebody walking over it.

On a Big Scale, Quick

Kerosene cans, wash tubs, wash boilers—even a plugged bath-tub—for a large number of people. Boil slowly, skim often, and let only one man use the salt. "Too many cooks spoil the broth."

One usually unforeseen difficulty in cooking in deep and big vessels is the weight or pressure at the bottom. This makes burning all too easy. To avoid this use a long wooden paddle and keep churning the mess. Here a trench is advisable to steady your heat. The gas pipe range shown in the plan is rigged on bent irons and men who have adopted this style of "Big Cookery" swear by it, both for wash boilers and roasting pans.

The Bath Tub Stew for a multitude! Don't crack the enamel and skim and *paddle,* or it will burn sure and be useless as food. Notice the plug *away from* the flames.

THE BATH-TUB STEW

Cyclone or Hurricane Soup would be safer than stew, perhaps.

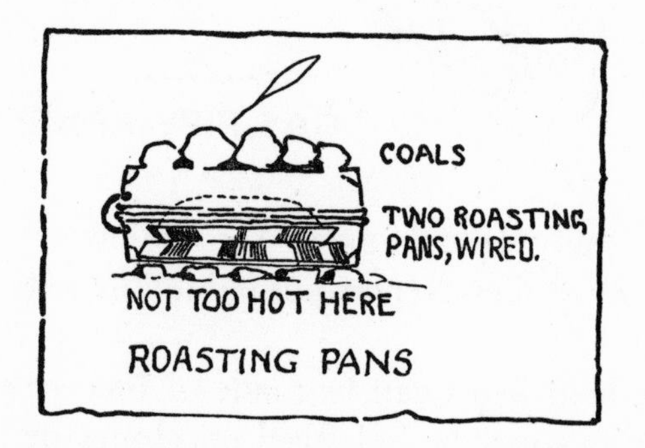

ROASTING PANS

For Corn bread! Or hot biscuits the combination has worked *miracles.*

Roasting Pans. These may be found with covers or another pan may be balanced or wired to go over the bottom pan, bottom up. In this anything can be cooked on a small or big scale. (Two boys once turned out 100 chupatties in one hour, 20 minutes, in this contrivance, while two more cooked 100 Hamburger steaks at the same time.)

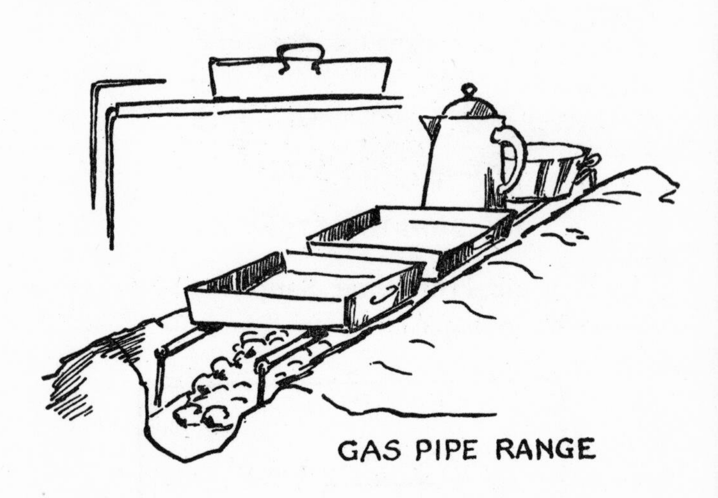

GAS PIPE RANGE

You may trench as in the diagram—or use bricks or stones—(non-poppable) or iron water pipes.

The bent irons can be made of fence-wire—or your pipes can be balanced on stones or bricks. This is a real "herd" kitchen and works to perfection.

The Cider-barrel Clam bake. Bore some holes in the bottom of a clean cider-barrel. Alternating with layers of seaweed, fill the barrel with, first, a layer of corn in the husk, then sweet potatoes, then chickens (nicely cleaned and tied up—perhaps stuffed with sea-weed)—then lobsters and crabs, lastly clams, oysters, or mussels. As in the

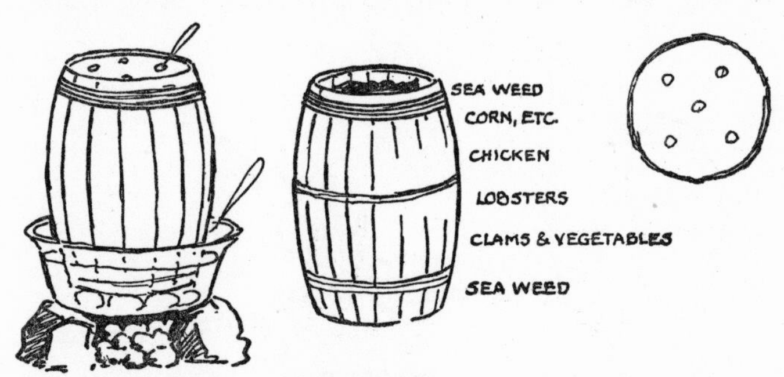

CIDER BARREL CLAM BAKE

diagram set your barrel holes up in a wash-tub of boiling water. The hot steam comes up through the various things—and when the clams are cooked the potatoes and chicken are done—say one hour and a half, maybe more. This is a "ship-wreck" affair—for a crowd of hungry people, but you may, some day, try it out with a very small cider-barrel, for a few starving pals.

To Boil Water in a Hogshead. Given a hogshead (for here a lot of hot water is wanted) and a length of water pipe—the longer the better.

Drive one end of the pipe in the bung, caulking it with a rag. In the other end drive a plug of soft wood, which must be whittled to fit. This plug is a safety-valve and is lower down than the bung end. If it blows out, drive it back in again. The hogshead being full of water, and no leaks in your bung or plug, build a roaring fire along the middle part of the pipe. The rising

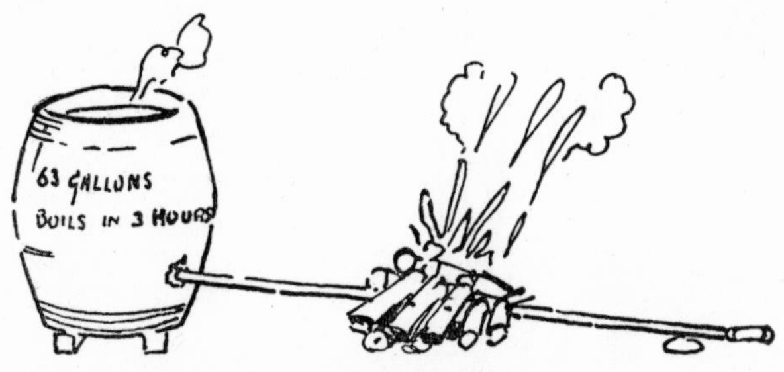

HOT WATER IN A HOGSHEAD
63 GALLONS IN A FEW HOURS

steam will heat the water in the hogshead in about two hours—in the summer, and will boil *in time.* Used for disinfecting or washing clothes. It makes a big noise while at work but is not dangerous on that account.

Throw me a line, quick!

Two men and a woman on a cake of ice drifting to a certain death in the rapids—somewhere on the River St. Lawrence. Men and women on the bridge see them coming! Panic! Shouts of

"Throw them a line! Get ropes, quick." Consternation! Ropes are found and dangled from above—there was time to do this—and the humans seem to be saved. What happened? Three naked lines swing before three pairs of half-frozen hands. A naked rope to stiffened fingers? Only the boy managed to grasp his line and swing clear of the ice. Those above began to hoist him to safety. But he couldn't hang on to this bare rope and dropped off. All three went over the rapids and were lost.

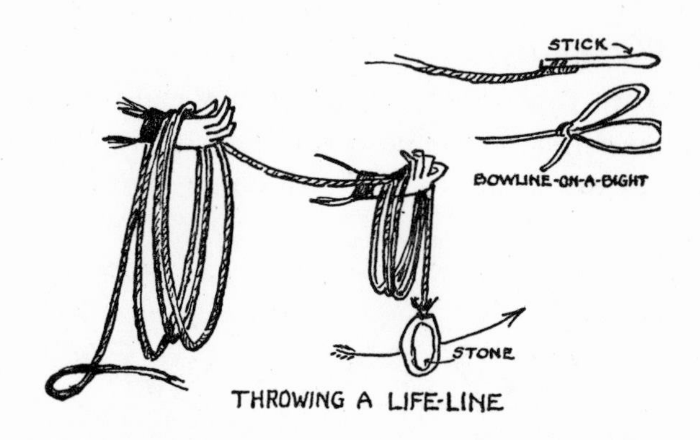

THROWING A LIFE-LINE

Moral: Learn *the Biggest Knot Known.* "Bowline-in-a-bight," it is called. It makes two loops (bights) in the end of a line big enough to slip under the arms or to thrust the legs into. A bare rope is usually useless as a life line *unless it has some sort of loop or stone or stick to hang on to.*

Throwing a rope or line.

Coil three bights in the right hand, leave about a yard free and then coil the balance of the rope and hold it lightly in your *left* hand. Then throw the right coil (the end tied with a bowline-in-a-bight)—and . . . see if you can throw the whole rope outwards as far as the rope will reach.

Practise this!

Tie the bow-line, throw the life-line against time as a game. Be ready!

The Old Kerosene Can.

Here you see what a smart boy can make out of an empty kerosene can. These cheap outdoor stoves are much in evidence on the frontiers of

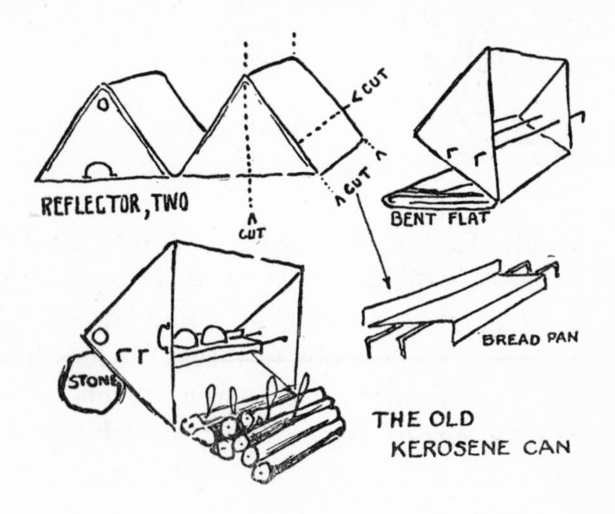

our land where the electric bulb has not yet penetrated.

The reflector needs a pair of tin cutting shears or a stout can opener and a length of fence-wire but it will turn out baked biscuits, fish or fowl in quick order. The fire must be built up in front

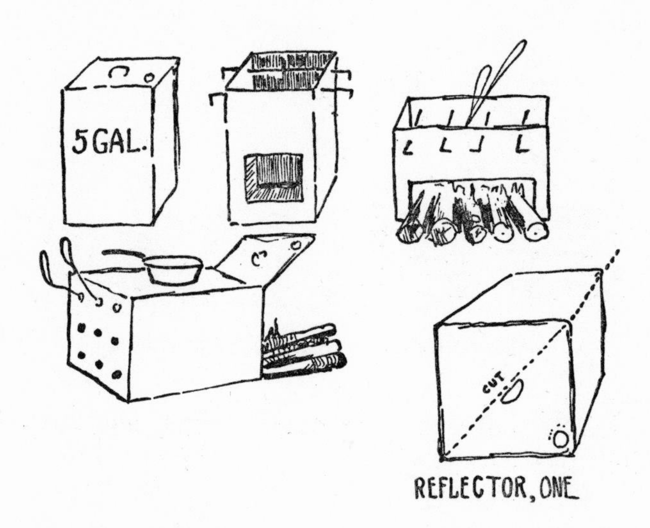

REFLECTOR, ONE

of the contraption, as shown in the sketch. One section must be flattened out as a base after cutting out a strip of tin for the bread pan. By piling the top and sides of an uncut can with coals and ashes, a man-sized loaf of bread may be baked as well as in the electric oven at home.

The Gold-Miner's Reflector Oven.

Invented, but not patented, by my father in the days of '49.

An arrangement of bright tin plate, fry-pan, shepherd's crook, with leaves still on the end, forked stick and a stone.

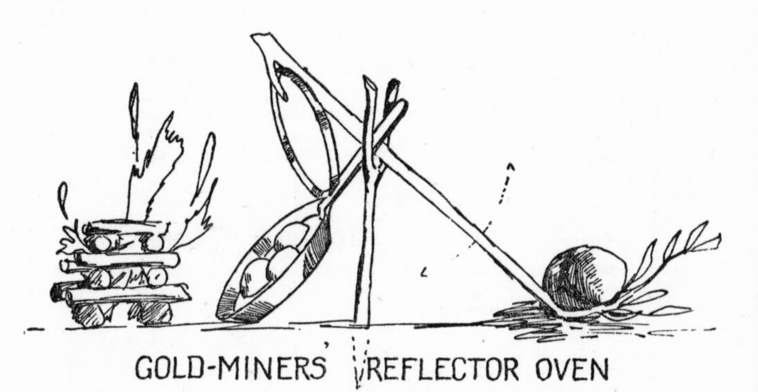

GOLD-MINERS' REFLECTOR OVEN

Flamey fire and dropped (wet) chupatties (big flap-jack).

Clay-baking.

Be sure that your clay is "sweet," that is, not odoriferous, for some clay or mud smells, and cooking in it taints the bird or fish, making it unfit to eat. Knead to a putty-like softness, then smear your feathered bird or your unscaled fish in it 3/4 inch deep. Bury in the coals; then, laid in the open air P. W. W., and covered with coals you bake until, by *guesswork* (after experiment, remember!), you may crack off the hardened clay taking jacket of feathers, skin and all—or fish skin-scales and all—with it. It is a picturesque way! See if you can rub the clay into the feathers so as to keep them well buried—else, sometimes, your pigeon, chicken, grouse, pheasant, prairie-hen, young turkey or (desperate!) your seagull will taste of wet feathers. Fish cooks quickly so use less clay on these.

Don't forget to rub salt *inside* your bird or fish.

See page 49 for this " dodge."

Emergency Illumination.

Put strips of birch bark in an old pry-top tin can, punch a small hole in the lid, then set it on a bed of coals. Then light the hole. It burns like an electric light—for a while.

Lights. A shell, a bit of fibre, and oil, grease, tallow-wax, grease *and* wax. I suppose this was the lamp of the caveman before he learned to harden clay by fire. I dug up a Greek lamp once, on Capri, and rigging a wick, poured olive oil into it. It burned again after three thousand years! It made a clear, bright light—good enough to read by!

Here are some **Emergency** *Lamps.*

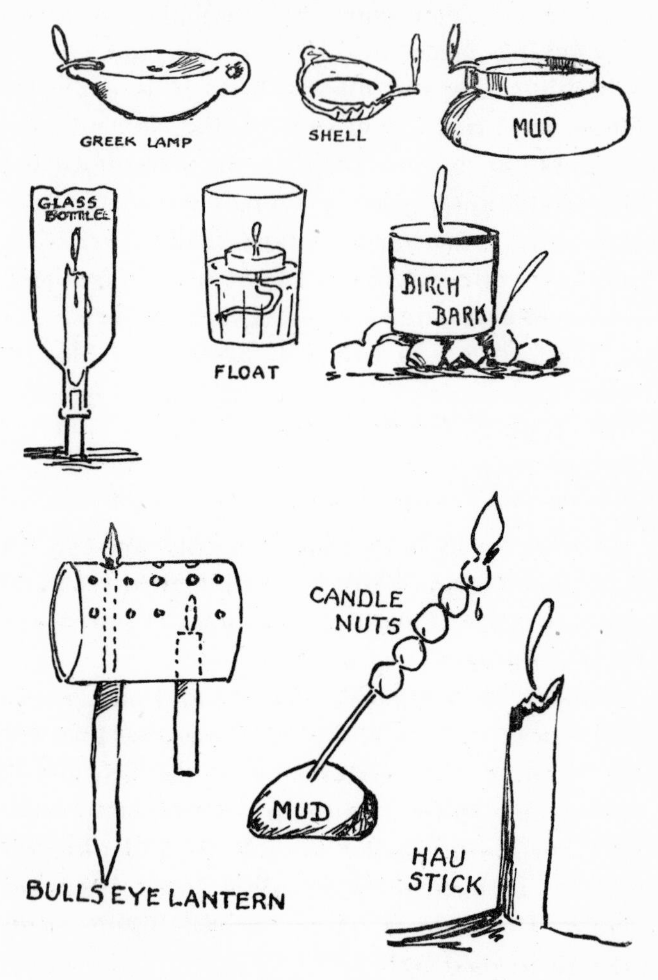

Glass bottle. To snap off the bottom, set it on your bed of coals for an instant. Then douse it into cold water. A pointed stake and a candle—and there you are. Wind proof.

Punched tin can—a bull's-eye lantern.

The Float. This is a night lamp, good for many hours.

In Hawaii the ends of dust-dry Hau branches, set alight and stuck up around your camp will smoulder all night with a fitful glow, occasionally emitting a stream of sparks (look out!) which discourages stray dogs and mosquitoes.

The paraffin candle is the cheapest. In a can—see bull's-eye—in a bottle—stuck into a mudball, into a hollowed-out potato. In a perforated tomato can.

Go to bed early and you won't need a light!

In the South Seas is found the candle-nut tree. During maneuvers near Honolulu in 1911, between the Red and Blue armies (where I was an "official observer") and where the Reds took Honolulu after we, the Blues, had killed, on paper, the Commanding General of the Reds six times, I showed a signal officer how to make a *kukui* or *candle-nut* torch. Under most "kukui" trees are found these ebony-black nuts. The old ones are oily and smelly. These you crack between stones and string on the midrib of a cocoanut leaf. Then you merely light the top one. This burns and makes a wonderful flame. Each nut lasts about 10 minutes and lights the next. The signal officer was much impressed and wrote it all down in his note book.

Another Frying-Pan Dodge.

Drop spoonsful of dough, wetter than for twisters, on a fry-pan, using no grease. Let rest on the coals until well stuck to the pan. Then when "set," tilt the pan upside down over the coals for a nice brown. "Painting" the buns at this last stage with milk or water helps to brown them.

This is Top Notch Camp Cookery and takes a great deal of practice.

ANOTHER FRYING PAN DODGE

Planking.

"Planking" is pinning your split-open fish, fowl, etc., on a slab of wood with wooden pegs, then tilting it over a hot bed of coals. Has this advantage: You can watch it at all stages.

On page 49 you have the picture.

ONE FATHOM

The Jack-knife Scale.

One inch: Measure your finger joints until you find one an inch long.

One span: An "octave"—from tip of thumb to tip of middle of little finger. My "span" is just nine inches. Measure and remember *yours*. Measure often until you stop growing!

One cubit: From elbow to finger tip.

One yard: From tip of nose to finger tip.

One fathom: Arms' length.

One pace: A stride—going.

Double pace: Two strides. Marked by the heels of your right foot. About five feet. Different for each boy or man.

Cooking Scale.

1 fistful = ½ cup.

1 5-finger pinch = ½ teaspoon.

1 3-finger pinch = ⅛ teaspoon.

7 to 10 "handfuls" of water = 1 tea-cupful.

Differs for each man or boy.

Helps you to "guess right."

Jack-knifer's Clock.

Throw the shadow of your thumb on your first finger held horizontally and stiff. Check this often with a clock or watch and remember the *changing* seasons.

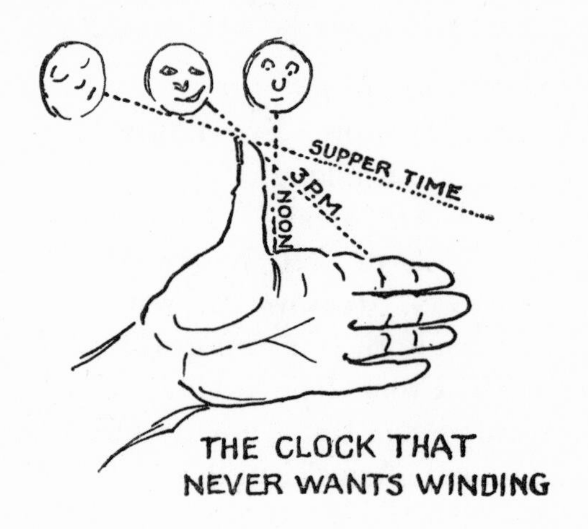

THE CLOCK THAT NEVER WANTS WINDING

Trespassing.

If only there were no Bedouins! But the owners of lands (pastures green, and bosky glades) are fed up with these dirty rascals. They have lost hens, eggs, and heartily object to the mess and filth *most campers* leave behind. And no wonder! Plan ahead—ask permission—if you can. When the farmer learns that you are "scientific" and a "William Appledip" which you can demonstrate to him easily enough, he'll probably say "All right, you can stay. But I won't have none o' them pesky Bedouins here." Then when you have oiled the pump, swept the veranda, or "porch"—and planted some fancy nasturtium seeds (15 cents per packet) Mrs. Farmer will probably give you a doughnut. And you have filled a ditch for the next "Jack-knifer."

How far is it to Samarkhand? How far is it from *here* to *there?* Ten miles? Use your wits—after reading the following:

SIGNALLING

The Outdoor Signalling Alphabet

With this alphabet mistakes are reduced to a minimum.

Thin, short, white, small, single things are DOTS.

Fat, long, black or colored, big, or double things are DASHES.

Dot is right. Dash is left. Down in Front is PERIOD.

The figure one or "1" is thin, and with a flag on a stick is made by a wave to the RIGHT. "Yes, dot is right."

Figure two, "2," is fat, double, and is made by a wave of the flag to the LEFT.

Now study this alphabet for ten minutes and you will be able to reconstruct it a year from now.

Four columns of seven letters each. Notice the headlines.

AHOV . . . which sounds like SHIP AHOY!
DKRY . . . begins the four unit or four numbered waves. Think of *Dickory*.

The GNU . . . that bewhiskered bull of the African plains.

A—11	H—12	O—21	V—22
B—111	I—121	P—211	W—221
C—112	J—122	Q—212	X—222
D—1111	K—1211	R—2111	Y—2211
E—1112	L—1212	S—2112	Z—2212
F—1121	M—1221	T—2121	&—221
G—1122	N—1222	U—2122	the—2222

See how it goes? 11, 12, 21, 22! AHOV is the key, but a little study will make you a signaller.

I've tried to remember the Morse code and gave it up as a bad job.

This funny alphabet has STUCK in my head for years . . . 11, 12, 21, 22. . . . Ahov and Dickory! If we taught this in the Army every private would be able to signal!

You may use pebbles in the road, knots on a string, toots on a whistle, notches in a twig, taps on a telephone, lantern in a bucket . . . scores of ways. It is always safe to use "period" or a space or pause between words, two for a sentence, three for the Very End.

Send P for a proposal, Q for a question, and in a really bad scrape, of course, but NEVER in fun, S-O-S, or O-O-O!

See *Outdoor Signalling*, by Elbert Wells, Macmillan, New York.

Organizing a Gang

When eight boys are gathered together they become a problem. Here begins the "herd" or tribe. Here there must arise a *leader,* otherwise the "crowd" splits up into a *mob*—all after something interesting, exciting, instructive (maybe) with *fun* in it, and not getting anywhere!

The "lone-wolf" idea becomes the "patrol-idea" when a bunch wants to play *together*. The world is filling up. When the young porcupine of today wants to huddle with his fellows, to keep warm, say, he must learn to smooth down his quills. The gang must *organize* or split. History is chuck full of experiments. The Egyptians, the Greeks, the Romans—all had a whack at "organization," wanting to get the most out of each other, for some object—usually "safety," peace, plenty.

The Jack-knifers, the Appledip's, Scouts, Seascouts, Demolays, Knights of Columbus—in fact, any sort of a gang of boys *with a code* (No Bedouins, please) might try this way. You may call it, this style of organization, any name you like. The Scouts call it "Pine Tree" and find a good, patient, healthy man to help them carry out certain *plans*. He is the "Blue" Print, the "Umpire" and devises, thinks out things, decent boys are usually crazy to do! To go camping!

To form a recreation club. To become Scouts! To club together and *do* something interesting: —build a cabin or a swimming hole—no matter what. You must de-mob-ilize. You must organize!

As you cannot do anything as a *mob*—you may adopt this plan and change it to fit your needs. It has worked well, when undertaken with *resolution* for twelve years now, all over the States and in Europe.

Under their "old-man" (over twenty-one, some say—over 45 is better) these boys organize a "patrol."

Here is the "scheme":

The Old Man. A tired business man who has a few hours to give to his country. (Ethan Allen, and a million others gave *all* their hours.) Only a few from you, Old Man!

Split the eight boys into two groups, Reds and Blues. Fall them in like a U. S. Army "squad."

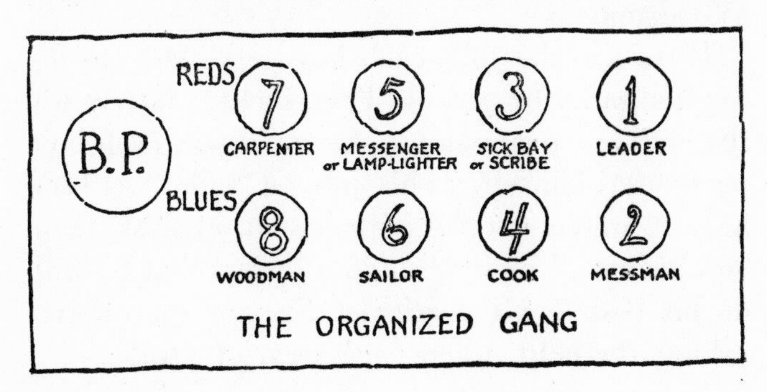

THE ORGANIZED GANG

Give this gang a *name*. "Bulls" will do—being the best-looking, stupidest animal in the menagerie! But brave, you bet, and husky!

The Reds. Bull One is a leader and that is to say he has earned the place, where he works, with his *brains,* and not so often with his *hands. He* represents the old man; the Blue Print. He is chosen, not for age or size or muscle but for coolness, brains and character. (Most boys want the best baseball player. "Well, that's a good way too." Find him.) He "heads" the whole patrol. He "learns" leadership by practise—a game some boys and some men never *can* learn. "Two" Bull, heads the rear rank, or Blues, subject to Bull One. *The Reds,* Number One, Three, Five and Seven are *specialists* and hold their places permanently, as a rule, because we need their special training. "Leader, Scribe, Lighter, Carpenter."

The Blues. Messman, Cook, Sailor and Woodsman.

Here are the jobs each boy gets ready to do for his gang, or patrol. They include nearly all the civilized professions—as you'll see, each boy *perfecting* himself, in his job, or "billet" as best he can, under careful supervision, at first, then "on his own," *under standing orders* that he will do his best *in his particular line* for the others, asking for help, when necessary, of course.

It's all for one—the Bulls—and one for all! Most boys realize that no gang or business, or ship, or country has more than one Blue Print or Constitution. That all of us cannot be the *leader*—that we, each of us, must fill our "billet," and *deliver the goods*—Every one in his place. For the benefit of the others and ourselves. A boy can be made to realize that his Bull Patrol is only an epitome (hard word, "sample" "specimen") of that greater patrol—his country! On this small scale in the gang or patrol we can divide the work, just as does a department store or as the United States does—finding men who are best fitted to fill certain posts *for the business in hand* and judging them by and honoring them for the *results.*

Here are these "billets" explained more fully. The Reds, under Bull One take over housing, cover and clothes. That includes tents, blankets, ponchos and duffle bags. *Responsible!* The Blues, under Two Bull (and One Bull) take over Provisions. This includes wood, water, food supply and meals. Subdividing *responsibilities* further, let us discuss these billets some more.

Bull One, the foreman of the working party, overlooks all and watches the Old Man for orders! (Scoutmaster, Seascout, Skipper, Sachem, Chief—whatever his organization calls him) who acts as the Big Brains of the business.

Bull One must encourage, check, urge—but work towards a perfectly harmonious working of this plan. It takes some care at first, for there are sudden overlappings and interferences that must be smoothed out, somehow, with great patience. *Bull Three* keeps records. A journal, accounts, money. Other names for him are Librarian, Bookkeeper, Banker, Pay-Clerk.

But I have added another set of billets to Number Three. He is also "Sick Bay," Hospital Steward, First Aid—We choose him for neatness. To keep him clean (and as an offset reward for much clerical work) he is excused from soiling duties. You'll say "A dude? A lounge Lizard?" Not at all! Safety-first—*scientific!* Sanitary!

Bull Five is assigned the illumination, hence "Lamp-Lighter." Oil, Candles, Carbide. Then, by analogy, electric lights! Wire, wireless, telephone; then *Messenger,* his most active job. Add signalling, radio, the Flag, and the packing of a small tool box for repairing lights of all sorts, in camp. Bull Seven is a Handyman with carpenter's tools. If he isn't much of a hand at it *teach* him. All wood-work is his province—something simple but good, following the old adage "Measure right, saw straight, nail straight, and come out right." You understand that he is, in a way, a sub-leader in his billet and must supervise and teach his pals? So with all billets—make each boy the master of his job and he will help all the others to acquire skill. No trade secrets in the Bulls.

The Blues

Bull Two buys the grub. Studies the food market—somebody must, for our finances may be very low! Arranges the *Menus.* A hard job, on which a whole army moves, as Bull Napoleon said, erstwhile leader of a very rambunctious patrol! He supervises the timely eats and the irksome wash up. Let him study this in some domestic science school—dishwashing! (It was agreed in the laboratory where this system was first tried that dishwashing was an "All hands" job where Bull Two is merely *boss. Responsible!*)

Bull Four is the most important martyr in our patrol. He must be petted, respected—taught, and once expert in seven good "bills-of-fare" can be given some very rare privileges. *The best seat in a movie,* for instance, worked in one case, I remember. Just for that foolish privilege, Bull Four would slave uncomplainingly for hours over a stew, the towel-washing, the fire! But at the play he chose and was given the *best seat,* even before the Old Man, and quite right! Bull Six. Sailor, waterman, life-saver (taught, by an expert to do Shaeffer's Prone Method); boats; at swimming hole, *boss*. Bull Six yells "All out"—and they must come, for Bull Six must be obeyed. By analogy he knows Filters, Ice Hole; "Good drinking water here"—and fishing and the fish. That's his job—but he is strong and helps all along the line, when wanted. Of course! Carries Sailorman's Kit bag; needles, wax, fid, twine, palm, etc.

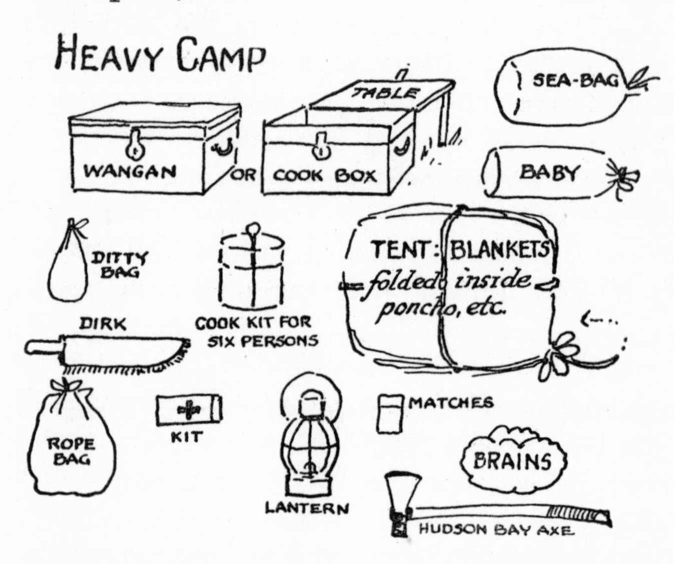

Bull Eight. Woodsman: chops wood, knows the trees, is an amateur botanist, and general out-door man! Carries and cares for our most dangerous tool, the Boy Slaying Axe. All rough-stuff like black-smithing comes under the billet.

For a patrol of eight, a real axe is necessary—and Bull Eight *alone* may wield it, being most carefully trained for the job, until he reports his pals, one by one, safe axe-men. ***Responsible!***

What now? Why camp, of course! See how quick things will move, after some training at home.

For the hand-cart camp, with two-boy tents, and a lot of "fancy" drills, 44 in number (Hospital, Ferry, Kitchen, Big Camp, etc.); for four patrols, ask any Scoutmaster to lend his "Pine Tree Patrol" book. Or buy one from Scout Headquarters. Or join the Scouts!

Water

Water in the Desert Island. "Robinson Crusoe" Charlie Gay got caught in the forest on *Mauna Loa,* a mountain on the Island of Hawaii, and having no water saved himself and his wife by squeezing the dew out of moss. "It was muddy," he told me, "but it tasted like Nectar of the Gods." Hikikoke, my cousin, while once crossing a spur on this same mountain, above the timber-line, was "all in" for want of water, when suddenly his broncho began to show signs of intelligence "surpassing strange." Hiki then and there discovered a great crevasse in the lava, ten feet under the crust, where there was a steady drip of water. He filled his hat and gave his horse to drink (Good Appledip!) and after slaking his thirst filled his canteen. In this place he found some calabashes and a wooden trough all gone into decay—showing that the ancient Hawaiians knew this hole—this oasis—in the waterless lava-desert. Years afterwards he tried to locate it but couldn't find it. Found and lost again—to be re-discovered by some future explorer. Moral: trust the Mustang.

Mr. Maxwell, late Territorial Forester in Hawaii, was once lost in the Never Never Desert in Queensland, North Australia. He had twice *vomited,* and was unable to speak, his tongue being so swollen, and kept going "off his head" with thirst. He lay down in the shade of a rock to die. While awaiting *death* he saw a lone wild duck fly overhead. He took a bearing of the duck's course on his pocket compass—followed that line to a water hole! Hurrah! Saved! If you ever get lost in the Never Never and are out of water look for a place where the blacks, the Australian Aborigines, have made a fire. Dig down and you may find some Emu's eggs filled with water. These are buried under an old fire to baffle the thirsty white man—but all Bushmen know the secret now. So do you!

HUSKING AND CUTTING OPEN A COCONUT

In the South Seas, the blessed coconut helps us out. Most people punch a hole in the "Monkeys Eyes" and so get at the coconut *water*. The Kanakas tackle the other end. Husking a coconut is done on a pointed stake. Drive the stake —sharpen it afterwards with your dirk. Then bash the nut on the pointed stake and wrench off the husk. With one blow of your dirk cut off the *sharp* end of the nut—it is easy with a green nut—and drink your fill. If you are *a-thirst*—no native of the Pacific Islands will begrudge you a green coconut.

Water in Tree-ferns.

These grow quite high but find a small one and chop out the heart of the tree. About two tablespoons of water will appear in a few minutes. Keep 10 trees going.

In Banana Stumps.

Cut down bananas and stack the trunks in a pail. The sap is bitter but better than nothing. I like it!

Here is a way to catch water for cooking purposes—on a real Robinson Crusoe's isle! Split a young, green, coco leaf down the middle, tie it around the stump with the stem leading into a coco shell. Always there are plenty of these shells lying about. That night, when it rains, if it does, the rain-water will trickle down the trunk of the tree and lead off into the nut. At Ascencion, in 1897 (Los Islas Marianas, look it up) we found this way of catching rain water.

FOR THE BEST BUN

I say "we." We followed the wise Kanakas! This book represents many a bold theft of ideas from all over the world as you, no doubt, have guessed.

I think the World is willing to give us new ideas—to use in our own way, if we *want* them.

Jack-Knifers are allowed to take what they need, ideas, "dodges," from all races, all civilizations. And we'll swap—like good sports.

But to resume:

Yarn No. 9

The story of *Palapala.* He was the engineer of a decked-over gasoline motor-boat, and had come to anchor off Mahukona.

His son went ashore, in the small boat, for more gasoline, water and provisions, while Palapala went below to clean the engine. He had been on the job for two hours when he came on the deck for fresh air. Anchor rope had parted! Land was almost out of sight and a gale blowing! With no gas, sail, oars, food or water. Palapala was reported lost and steamers and Power sampans were sent out to find him. Which they did ten days later. I knew old Palapala and this is how he "Robinson Crusoed" for food and water. He rigged a tarpaulin by the four corners on his forward deck, with an iron spanner in the middle, where he punched a hole in the canvas Arranged a bucket under it. Then prayed for rain. That came on the second night! For food he fashioned a hook out of wire. For bait he made a "wobble-spoon" of tin and tied a red rag on it at the end of a fish line, made from unravelled strands of rope, and "spun" on his thigh, native style. Trolling with this he was lucky enough to hook a twenty-five pound Ono or "Pacific Ocean Mackerel"! He dried pieces of this on the deck for future use—and—there you are! Hero! Jack-knifer!

Moral: Never say die!

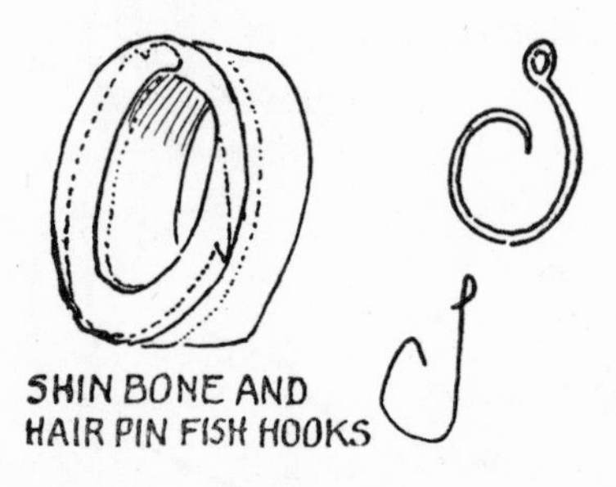

Then there were once two women and a man left three days on an islet off the coast of England. Their boat got adrift—a fog came down and when rescued they were all three so done in with hunger and exposure that the man and one woman died. Now I ask you what would you have done? No fish line? How make one? No fish hook or bait (for a couple of fish eaten raw are better than nothing).

How make one? Well, here is a good place to show you the time-honored (in the Pacific) hook of Mawi and the daily "Sennet" or Kaula. Had this Englishman known what follows—and had he had some training in his grand-father's back garden (our Desert Island, our Robinson Crusoe's Isle, where we try all these things as in a physical and chemical laboratory or workshop) he would have deserved a better fate.

Prince Kuhio Kalanianaole, for twenty years Hawaii's Prince-delegate to Congress, a friend of my school days, refused to fish with a barbed fish-hook. He preferred the ancient Polynesian type. It can be made out of a *hair-pin* by bending as in the diagram. Kuhio claimed this hook to be superior to the "store kind" for it somehow catches in a fish's upper lip. Now for a fish line. An unravelled stocking—preferably silk! You must learn how to spin two strands on your bare thigh or leg (practise it in the bath-room at first) as do the amiable Samoans, Fijians, Tahitians, Tubutaians—in fact, all the men of the South Seas are expert at this *Sennet spinning*. Try it first with flax, oakum, wool or cotton or an "unlayed" (unravelled) piece of rope—which is usually sisal or banana fibre.—Pick the rope apart. This is "Spunyarn" and will twist into very strong fish line—if you know how. Dried coco husk, pounded between two stones until the fibres separate, is the best stuff to use. You feed the new fibres in as you go, and roll up your twine as it is spun out. Excellent substitute for a fancy priced fish-line. Study the sketch. What bait could he have used? Barnacles, limpets, a bit of his cravat, a minnow caught in a pool.

Along the North Coast of Africa at low tide, and I *suppose* in other places, is the much prized *sand worm,* at about six inches deep. If you are cast away *there* don't forget this information. In the mangrove swamps of the East Indies prawns are easily caught. Remember the man who used a butterfly wing as a bait? Use your wits—*now,* before you get into the predicament of being Cast Away on a Desert Island!

HOBO SAUCEPAN
+
THE TOMATO CAN! *The last straw for the hungry.* SPAGHETTI, RICE, STEW, FRIED THINGS. *Be sure it is* SURGICALLY CLEAN.

Get used to being "cast away"! It means *casting away* a lot of very useful truck: rat-traps, dancing pumps, but never your tooth brush, or your Jack-Knife!

Pretend to be lost once in a while and so get *used* to it. See what you can do with little to do

with and get an "education" that may help you in other ways. To be a Jack-Knifer takes brains and that other wonderful attribute: imagination. And ever so often—crash!—the time comes when you *must* do it—Then why not know *how?*

This ***Wikiup*** at bottom of preceding page is a case in point. Will it *work?* Go ahead and try it.

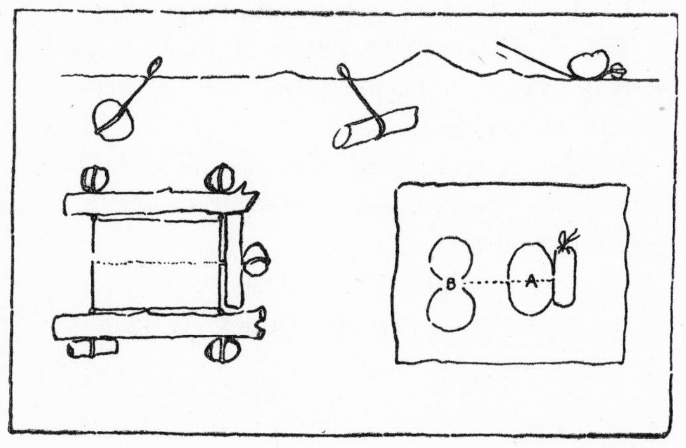

"Dead Men" and Hip and Shoulder Holes, in Sand

The above tries to show some "dead men" for a *sandy site* and a scheme for a sand bed. Head mark (pillow?), shoulder holes (A) and hip holes at B (usually three spans from A). Remember to spread your poncho, rain coat, slicker, or ground cloth, and a blanket and avoid the chill that comes up into your spine, from the damp sand. No matter how dry it *feels,* or looks.

Camping, cooking, sleeping on the beach—On the sand! It does sound romantic, somehow, but tents blow down and sand works its way into the food, if you don't take pains. Keep to leeward of your "kitchen" and steady your tent with "many inventions."

Envoy!

I believe this means the end and goodbye.

This book is waste paper if it does not encourage boys to *Experiment*. Not always with gunpowder, either.

In the language of the people in this big Ocean, the Pacific, *Aloha Oukou a Pau!* My regards to you all!

Pine Tree Jim

(*Alias* James A. Wilder).